PIONEER
CATHOLIC HISTORY
OF OREGON

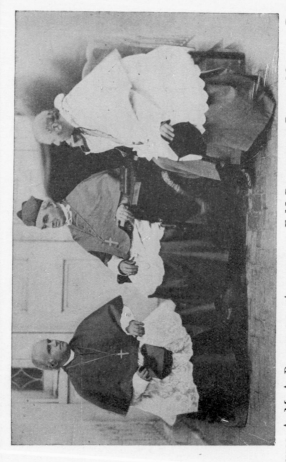

Bishop A. M. A. Blanchet   Archbishop F. N. Blanchet   Bishop Modeste Demers

The Founders of the Catholic Church in the Pacific Northwest

Pioneer CATHOLIC HISTORY *of* OREGON

By Edwin V. O'Hara

(CENTENNIAL EDITION)

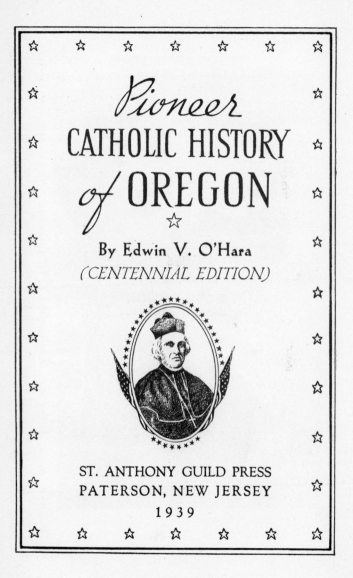

ST. ANTHONY GUILD PRESS
PATERSON, NEW JERSEY

1939

965

Imprimatur.

✠ Edwin V. O'Hara,
Bishop of Great Falls.

March 25, 1939.

TO

Most Rev. Edward D. Howard, D. D.

ARCHBISHOP OF PORTLAND IN OREGON

PREFACE TO FIRST EDITION

☆

This little book, the product of spare moments, has been written to help make better known the story of those Catholic pioneers of the Oregon Country whose names even now seem to be borne down to us from a distant heroic past. Blanchet, DeSmet and McLoughlin are the names of heroes. No prouder names are inscribed on the honor roll of pioneer missionaries and empire builders of the Western hemisphere. No effort has been made in these pages to pronounce an eulogy upon them; their best eulogy is a simple narrative of their lives and deeds.

The manuscript *Memoirs of Most Rev. F. N. Blanchet,* by Major Mallet and the large collection of Letters and Documents in the Archdiocesan Archives in Portland, have yielded much material here published for the first time. Other collections of *Oregoniana* which the writer has searched for items of Catholic interest are the Bancroft Collection at the University of California; Major Mallet's Collection (L'Union St. Jean-Baptiste d'Amerique, Woonsocket, R. I.); the Congressional Library, Washington, D. C.; the Shea Collection (Georgetown University Library), Washington, D. C.; the collection of the Oregon Historical Society, Portland; the Oregon History section of the Portland Public Library, and the splendid private collections of rare

Oregoniana of Mr. Frederick V. Holman, President of the Oregon Historical Society, and of Mr. Clarence B. Bagley, of Seattle. The writer is indebted to Mr. Clinton A. Snowden, of Tacoma, author of *The History of Washington,* and to Mr. John P. O'Hara, editor of the *Catholic Sentinel,* for revising proofs and making many valuable suggestions. Several chapters are reprinted, with permission, from the pages of the *Catholic University Bulletin,* the *Catholic World,* and the *Oregon Historical Quarterly.*

Portland, Oregon, September 6, 1911.

PREFACE TO SECOND EDITION

☆

The introductory and final chapters in the present edition are new; the letters of Father Croke have been compressed into one chapter (Chap. XVIII). The final chapter gives a summary sketch of the growth of the archdiocese from the retirement of Archbishop Blanchet to the present day. This extension of the narrative explains the omission of "pioneer" from the title of the book.

The author is grateful to the many kindly critics of the first edition and is indebted especially to Judge F. W. Howay for a painstaking review of the book in Vol. 17 of the *Review of Historical Publications Relating to Canada.*

EDWIN V. O'HARA

St. Mary's Cathedral, Portland.

Feast of Pentecost, 1916.

NOTE TO THIRD EDITION

☆

In this edition the History of the Catholic Church in Oregon is continued down to the death of Archbishop Christie and to the decision of the United States Supreme Court in the Oregon School Law case. With these events an era in Oregon Catholic History closes.

EDWIN V. O'HARA

Newman Hall.

Eugene, Oregon.

Feast of Pentecost, 1925.

PREFACE TO CENTENNIAL EDITION

☆

The approaching centennial celebration of the Church in the Oregon Country provides an occasion for a fourth and final edition of this little book which still remains after nearly thirty years the only single volume account available of the more significant Catholic pioneers in the Pacific Northwest. It is earnestly to be hoped that some competent hand will soon give us a much more detailed picture of this interesting pioneer scene. I must express my appreciation of the kind reception which the historians of the Oregon Country have given the previous editions of this volume. To have the approving nod of Frederick V. Holman, Clinton A. Snowden, Judge F. W. Howay, Clarence B. Bagley and George Fuller in this field has been generous compensation for the labor of writing.

The present edition will show numerous changes and some important additions made necessary by more recent studies in the history of the Hudson's Bay Company in their London archives and also by research in the archives of the Archdiocese of Quebec. In this connection I again acknowledge the painstaking collaboration and criticism of my brother, Mr. John P. O'Hara, of Portland, Oregon.

I have thought best to have the title revert to that of the first edition, *Pioneer Catholic History of Oregon,* and to consign to an Appendix the brief account of the archdiocese following the death of Archbishop Blanchet. The chronology of the archbishops and bishops of the ecclesiastical province is added for convenience of reference. Finally, the bibliography (revised) of the first edition, and the index, give completion to the volume.

The Diocese of Great Falls, though not a part of the original jurisdiction of Archbishop Blanchet (lying, as it does, to the east of the Continental Divide) has, however, an interesting pioneer link binding it to Oregon, in that Father Croke, who built the first church in Portland (1851), was also the first priest to reside for a considerable time (the winter of 1855) at Fort Benton, the oldest white settlement in Montana.

✠ EDWIN V. O'HARA,
Bishop of Great Falls

Great Falls, Montana
March 1, 1939

CONTENTS

LIST OF ILLUSTRATIONS

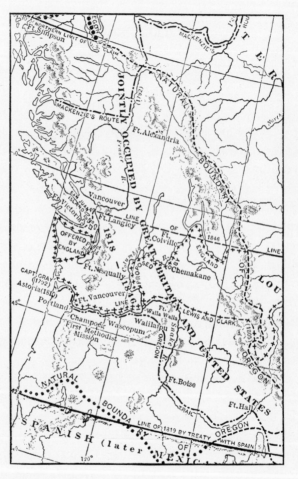

OREGON COUNTRY IN PIONEER DAYS (1792-1846)

INTRODUCTION

DISCOVERY AND EXPLORATION

1. Spanish and English Explorers.

The Oregon Country of pioneer history was a vast territory between the Rocky Mountains and the Pacific Ocean and extended from the present northern boundary of California and Nevada to Alaska. The Northwest coast had been explored in 1774 by a Spanish expedition from Monterey under Juan Perez, and in the following year another Spaniard, Heceta, while sailing along the Oregon coast, discovered the mouth of the great "River of the West," but did not enter. Father Magin Catala and other Franciscan missionaries accompanied these exploring voyages and met the Indians at Nootka Sound, but left no permanent establishment and exerted no influence on the natives.

While the American Revolution was in progress the famous English explorer, Captain James Cook, visited the Oregon coast and revealed to the world the hitherto unsuspected commercial possibilities of the Northwest. His ships were visited by the savages, who offered great supplies of otter skins in exchange for gaudy trifles. On reaching China, Cook's crew found an extraordinary demand for the skins — "Skins which did not cost the

1

purchaser sixpence sterling sold for one hundred dollars." Oregon was now on the map commercially and before long traders from the leading nations were establishing relations with the Oregon Indians for the profitable barter of furs.

2. American Claims Established.

After the American Revolution a small vessel, the Columbia, fitted out by Boston merchants, plied between the Oregon coast and China, in charge of Captain Robert Gray. In 1792, on a tour along the coast, Gray entered the mouth of the river, the existence of which had been noted by Heceta in 1775. This was the River of the West, the "Oregon" of the great traveler Jonathan Carver and the "Ouragon" of Major Robert Rogers of the famous Rogers' Rangers. Gray gave the river the name of his ship, the Columbia, and gave to America by his discovery and exploration a title to the "Oregon Country," of which the newly-discovered river was the chief commercial artery.

For twenty years before his election to the office of President, Thomas Jefferson, alone among American statesmen, took an intelligent interest in Oregon. On his accession to that office he bent his energies to establish American claims in the Northwest. In 1803 he addressed a message to Congress recommending that an exploring expedition be sent up the Missouri River and across the mountains "even to the Western ocean."

Under the command of Meriwether Lewis and William Clark, the expedition planned by Jefferson had penetrated to the summit of the Rockies by August, 1805, and began the descent of the western slope along streams whose waters found their way to the Pacific. The Pacific Ocean itself, at the mouth of the Columbia, they reached on November 7 of the same year and returned to St. Louis September, 1806, with news of their success in establishing a highway across the continent and in opening friendly relations with the Indians of the Rocky Mountains and the plains of the Columbia. The expedition of Lewis and Clark strengthened the claim of the United States to the Columbia River basin, a claim established by Gray's discovery of the river.

3. The Oregon Fur Trade.

The first quarter of the 19th century witnessed a struggle for control of the fur trade in the Oregon Country. The Hudson's Bay Company (chartered by Charles II in 1670), which ultimately captured the field, had the advantage of immense capital and thorough organization. The Northwest Company of Montreal, through the untiring energy and wonderful explorations of Alexander Mackenzie (1789-93) and Simon Fraser (1806), who discovered and explored the rivers which bear their names, obtained a foothold west of the Rocky Mountains.

On the return of Lewis and Clark with information concerning the possibilities of fur trade on the Columbia, John Jacob Astor, a New York merchant, who had long been engaged in the fur trade, decided to enter the new field. His first ship arrived at the mouth of the Columbia in March, 1811, and the crew, after many hardships, selected a site for a fort and founded the first American settlement in Oregon, giving it the name of Astoria. Astor's overland party arrived within a year with reinforcements for the new trading post of the Pacific Fur Company. Learning that the Northwest Company was actively establishing its trade connections among the Indians, the Astoria traders determined on an energetic campaign for control of the business. The year 1812 brought success to their efforts; but it also brought news of impending disaster. War was on between England and the United States. In October, 1813, the Americans sold out to the Northwest Company, and six weeks later a British warship entered the Columbia and took possession of Fort Astoria. The Northwest Company retrieved its position and controlled the Oregon fur trade until 1821, when the Northwest Company became merged in the Hudson's Bay Company. It was on the occasion of this coalition that Dr. John McLoughlin was sent to Oregon (1824) as chief factor of the Hudson's Bay Company.

4. Period of Joint Occupancy.

In 1818, a convention between Great Britain and the United States provided that the citizens and subjects of the two nations should have equal access to the Oregon Country for ten years. This arrangement was subsequently extended and it was not until 1846 that the northwest boundary was finally fixed. The years between 1818 and 1846 are known as the period of joint occupancy. It can be readily seen that the administrative problems arising under such conditions would be of an extremely delicate nature and would tax the highest executive powers. During this period the history of Oregon is largely the story of the life of Dr. John McLoughlin.

Dr. John McLoughlin — "Father of Oregon"

CHAPTER ONE

McLOUGHLIN AT FORT VANCOUVER

I. Early Years of McLoughlin.

McLoughlin was born October 19, 1784, in Parish
La Rivière du Loup, Canada, and was baptized on
November 3 of the same year. Both of his parents were
Catholics; his father of Irish, his mother of Scotch,
descent. The boy seems to have been reared in the
home of a maternal grandfather, who brought him up
in the Established Church of England. It is certain
that prior to the date of his conversion to the Catholic
faith in 1842 it was his custom at Fort Vancouver to
read the services of the English Church to the congregation of officers and employes who attended. The influence of a maternal uncle decided the boy to become
a physician. He made his studies partly in Canada and
partly in Scotland, and probably in France. In early
manhood he joined the Northwest Company and was
placed in charge of Fort William, the chief depot and
factory of the company, situated at the mouth of the
Kaministiquia River on the north shore of Lake Supe-

rior. Here he met and married the widow of Alexander McKay, a former partner of John Jacob Astor in the Pacific Fur Company. Their union was blessed with four children. Of their surviving descendants none perpetuates the name McLoughlin.

2. McLoughlin Becomes Chief Factor.

In 1821, when the Northwest Company was about to coalesce with the Hudson's Bay Company, Dr. McLoughlin as a partner in the former, strongly opposed the combination as unfair and prejudicial to the interests of his company. When the coalition had taken place, the Hudson's Bay Company officials in recognition of his executive ability appointed him Chief Factor of the company in the Oregon Country. McLoughlin came overland to Astoria in 1824 in company with George Simpson, later Governor-in-Chief of all the Hudson's Bay Company territories in North America. Simpson soon perceived that the great trading post should be located near the confluence of the Willamette and Columbia Rivers. Accordingly he founded Fort Vancouver on the north side of the Columbia River about seven miles above the mouth of the Willamette. In 1839 McLoughlin constructed a new fort at the distance of a mile from the original fort on the site of the present United States military barracks, known as Vancouver Barracks.

3. Relations With the Indians.

With his headquarters at Fort Vancouver, Dr. McLoughlin was Chief Factor of the immense commercial interests of the Hudson's Bay Company, in the midst of fifty thousand Indians. In a letter published in the *Oregon Spectator,* September 12, 1850, McLoughlin speaks of his relations with the Indians: "When the Hudson's Bay Company first began to trade with these Indians they were so hostile to the whites that they had to mount guard day and night at the establishment, having sentinels at the gates to prevent any Indian entering unless to trade, and when they entered to take their arms from them. The Columbia could not be traveled in parties of less than sixty well-armed men; but by the management of the company they were brought to that friendly disposition that two men for several years back can travel in safety between this (Oregon City) and Fort Hall." There were no Indian wars in the Oregon Country during the entire period of McLoughlin's administration at Fort Vancouver from 1824 to 1846. The first Indian war began with the Whitman massacre in 1847, the year after McLoughlin retired from the Hudson's Bay Company. Mr. Holman, in his biography of McLoughlin, rightly ascribes this remarkable fact to the commanding personality of the Chief Factor. He writes: "Physically, Dr. McLoughlin was a superb specimen of man. His height was not less than six feet four inches. He carried himself as a master, which gave him an appearance of being more than six feet and a half high. He was almost perfectly proportioned. Mentally he was endowed to match his magnificent physical proportions. He was brave and fearless; he was true and just; he was truthful and scorned to lie. The Indians, as well as his subordinates, soon came to know that if he threatened punishment for an offense, it was as certain as that the offense occurred. He was absolute master of himself and of those under him. He was *facile princeps*. And yet, with all these dominant qualities, he had the greatest kindness, sympathy and humanity." Shortly after his arrival in Oregon, McLoughlin, following the policy of his company, put a stop to the sale of liquor to the Indians. In 1834 a rival trader, named Wyeth, stopped selling liquor to the Indians at McLoughlin's request. A few years later an American vessel came to the Columbia River to trade, having a large supply of liquors. The Chief Factor prevented the sale of the liquor to the savages by buying up the entire quantity.

4. Hospitality at Fort Vancouver.

Fort Vancouver was a haven of peace for the early immigrants after their dangerous trip across the plains. All travelers who drifted into the Columbia River country found at the Fort a most hospitable welcome. Nathaniel Wyeth, whom we have instanced as a rival trader, came overland in 1832. His party arrived at Vancouver in a destitute condition. In Wyeth's *Journal,* under date of October 29, 1832, we read: "Arrived at the fort of Vancouver. Here I was received with the utmost kindness and hospitality by Dr. John McLoughlin, the acting Governor of the place. Our people were supplied with food and shelter. I find Dr. John McLoughlin a fine old gentleman, truly philanthropic in his ideas." On leaving Fort Vancouver in February, 1833, Wyeth writes the following entry: "I parted with feelings of sorrow from the gentlemen of Fort Vancouver. Dr. McLoughlin, the Governor of the place, is a man distinguished as much for his kindness and humanity as his good sense and information; and to whom I am so much indebted as that he will never be forgotten by me." And Wyeth was a competitor of the Hudson's Bay Company. Among others whose experience was similar to that related by Wyeth was the naturalist, Townsend, who came to the Fort in 1834. Writing of the reception his party met with at the hands of Dr. McLoughlin, Townsend says: "He requested us to consider his house our home, provided a separate room for our use, a servant to wait upon us, and furnished us with every convenience which we could possibly wish for. I shall never cease to feel grateful to him for his disinterested kindness to the poor, houseless and travel-worn strangers."

Most Rev. F. N. Blanchet
FIRST ARCHBISHOP OF OREGON CITY

CHAPTER TWO

THE FUTURE ARCHBISHOP OF OREGON

The Blanchet Family. — The Brothers at School. —
The Acadian Mission. — Schooled for an Arduous
Apostolate. — Celebrating the Feast of St. Ann. —
Life at Village of Cedars

1. The Blanchet Family.

It is a long journey from Miramichi Bay on the Gulf of St. Lawrence to the metropolis of Oregon, where the Willamette River mingles its waters with those of the great River of the West on its majestic course to the Pacific. And it were a long story to recount in detail the travels and labors of the Abbé Blanchet from his early missions among the peaceful Acadians and docile Micmac Indians of New Brunswick to his heroic work in planting the standard of the cross and establishing an ecclesiastical province in the Pacific Northwest. The subject of this chapter was born on September 3, 1795, in the parish of St.-Pierre, Rivière du Sud, Lower Canada. He was baptized on the following day at the neighboring village of St. Francois, receiving the Christian name of Francois probably in honor of the patron saint of the parish church in which the ceremony was performed. His parents, Pierre and Rosalie Blanchet, belonged to old Catholic families — many of the members of which had won honorable distinction in public life. A near relative of the future Archbishop, Francois Blanchet, M. D., was one of the founders of the first French Canadian newspaper, the celebrated *Canadien,* which was established to safeguard the civil and religious liberties of its countrymen. Another relative, a second cousin, Dr. Jean Blanchet, during the prevalence of the Asiatic cholera in 1832 and 1834, won the gratitude of thousands of Irish immigrants who arrived at the port of Quebec while that terrible plague was raging. The Blanchet family has also given many members to the Church. In a genealogical memoir we find the names of fifteen priests and an equal number of religious in communities of women.

2. The Brothers at School.

The young Francois and his brother Magloire, afterwards Bishop of the diocese of Walla Walla and subsequently, of Nesqually, were sent to the parish school in the village of St.-Pierre. The school was founded and directed by the pastor, Rev. Joseph Paquet, to prepare promising youth of his own and neighboring parishes for their classical studies. About the time that the two brothers entered, it was the custom for ecclesiastical students not in holy orders to be sent to the school from

Quebec as instructors in Latin. In its brief existence of a dozen years, St. Joseph's College (for so the school was properly called) was the nursery of a number of distinguished churchmen, a notable instance besides our two bishops being the future Archbishop of Quebec, Msgr. Charles Francois Baillargeon. The young Francois and Magloire Blanchet entered as day scholars, but the walk of four miles from their home to the school in the severe winter weather and especially the danger of crossing the river (Rivière du Sud) determined their parents to enter them as boarders. Francois made his First Communion in 1808 (in his twelfth year) and was confirmed the following year, adopting the name Norbert, which he afterwards used as a second Christian name. In 1810 the boys were sent to the minor Seminary of Quebec. During his classical and philosophical course, Francois won distinction in his studies; we find him carrying off first prize in Latin composition and the pompous title of "Imperator" (first honor) in a competition in Latin translation. In 1816 he entered the Superior Seminary of Quebec and after a distinguished theological course was ordained to the priesthood on July 19, 1819, and celebrated his first Mass on the following day. The ordination ceremony was performed by Bishop Panet, coadjutor to Msgr. Plessis, the illustrious Bishop of Quebec, during the absence of the latter in Europe.

3. The Acadian Mission.

During the year following his ordination the Abbé Blanchet was stationed at the Cathedral of Quebec as assistant. But Divine Providence, which had in store for him the arduous duties of a far Western apostolate, selected a more suitable and effectual preparation for his life's work. The old mission of St. Antoine of Richibucto, New Brunswick, becoming vacant, the Very Rev. Bernard Angus MacEachern, Vicar General and Bishop-elect for the Province and Islands of the Gulf, appealed to Msgr. Plessis to send him a French-speaking priest for the Acadians of that important mission. The lot fell upon the young Abbé Blanchet, who set out for his new field of labor in October, 1820. New Brunswick was formerly included in Acadia, the wrongs of whose people Longfellow has sung with so much pathos. The Micmac Indians were the original possessors of the land, but the French had been their neighbors for a century and a half. With the energy which characterized him throughout life, the Abbé Blanchet set about restoring the village church, establishing catechetical schools and founding choirs. The better to minister to the wants of his Irish parishioners, he undertook the study of English and soon began to instruct the children in that language. To the end of his life he was never weary of extolling the virtues of his Acadian flock.

4. Schooled for an Arduous Apostolate.

The vast territory under his charge was a wilderness without roads or bridges. "The Abbé Blanchet's mission, which was visited regularly at least twice a year, involved the travel of about 225 miles to reach the several stations, situated on rivers, bays and capes. In summer this was done in birch canoes along the rivers; in log canoes called pirogues, when crossing the arms of the sea; on horseback across the country, and in winter, on skates or snowshoes or in dog trains, and this in a region where the thermometer marks thirty degrees below zero and where for some months the earth and ice are covered with several feet of snow. The oldest inhabitants still tell (1880) of his heroism in storms and dangers of every kind; how he encouraged his good Acadian or Indian guides and shared with them their arduous labors and perils. His zeal never flagged, and after one of these long journeys to his distant stations, or after attending a sick call at a distance of a hundred or two hundred miles, he would return to his humble dwelling in the village as cheerful and joyous as did the Acadian farmer from his day's labor in his fields. Thus was the missionary being schooled for the duties of his apostolate in the wilds of distant Oregon." (Mallet, *Manuscript Memoirs of F. N. Blanchet,* p. 15.)

5. Celebrating the Feast of St. Ann.

A feature of missionary life among the Micmacs that appealed strongly to the Abbé Blanchet was the annual pilgrimage of the Indians to the shrine of St. Ann of the Burnt Church, which was an object of special devotion to all the neighboring tribes. At that hallowed spot on the northern shore of the great Miramichi Bay, the Indians of the whole surrounding country assembled annually to celebrate the feast of St. Ann on July 26. After weeks of elaborate preparation, the various tribes arrived from their respective homes. The Micmacs in their best garments and in their newly-painted pirogues, decorated with flags and banners, formed a flotilla and amid the firing of guns, with their missionary at their head, started on their long journey to the north. The arrival of the Richibucto delegation was the occasion of special demonstrations among the Indians of the Bay. Then came eight days of religious exercises and instructions under the direction of the pastor, Rev. Thomas Cook, afterwards Bishop of Three Rivers, Canada, ending with the general reception of Holy Communion on the feast of St. Ann. Scenes similar to this were to be common enough to our missionary in the Oregon Country.

6. Life at Village of Cedars.

In the spring of 1827, the Abbé Blanchet, after seven years of missionary labor among the Acadians, acceded to the request of an old friend, Mr. Lavignon, to accompany him to Quebec. On his mother's death in 1821, shortly after his arrival at Richibucto, his old home had been broken up, and hence he expected only temporary absence from his charge. His superiors decided otherwise and appointed him to the important parish of Cedars, or St. Joseph de Soulanges, in the Diocese of Montreal. The pleasant village of Cedars was not so much a center for a farming community as a rendezvous for boats passing up and down the river. It was a great resort for travelers and voyageurs. Here our missionary came in contact with the current of life that was moving towards the west. The fur trader and the adventurer who had dared the dangers of the Rocky Mountains and had come back with tales of the rich harvest to be won from trading with the western Indians were frequent visitors at the Cedars. Here, too, the heroism of the missionary was submitted to a severe test. In 1832 the dreadful scourge of cholera broke out in his parish and his ministration knew no lines of creed. It was at this time that the non-Catholics of the place presented him with two large and beautiful silver cups in token of their admiration for his conduct in visiting the sick and dying.

CHAPTER THREE

THE OREGON MISSION

Opening the Western Fur Lands. — Bishop Provencher at St. Boniface. — The Willamette Settlement
Requests Missionaries. — Mission Encouraged North
of the Columbia. — Missionaries Appointed for Oregon. — From Montreal to Fort Vancouver. — First
Mass at Fort Vancouver

I. Opening the Western Fur Lands.

We come now to the events which lead to the establishment of the Oregon mission. Up to 1731, although
the French possession and the diocese of Quebec were
presumed to extend into the interior to the uttermost
limits of the undefined West, the country beyond Lake
Superior and the headwaters of the Mississippi was still
unexplored. An expedition projected in that year under
the command of Pierre Gaulthier, Sieur de la Verendrye,
commandant of a post on Lake Superior, set out for the
West and ascended the Assiniboine and its tributary,
the Mouse River, in North Dakota. In 1742-1743 the
eldest son of La Verendrye led a small party ascending
the upper Missouri or one of its tributaries. They were
the first white men to discover the Rocky Mountains.
The country thus opened up became the great fur land

of North America. Beside the fort of the trader soon
arose the log house of the colonist. When Canada
passed into the hands of England in 1763, French settlements were to be found on the Red River, on Lake
Manitoba and even on the mighty Saskatchewan. The
Hudson's Bay Company soon opened its forts in the
new regions, and the Canadians, unable to maintain
an unequal contest, retired to lower Canada. The organization of the Northwest Company in 1776, however, once more gave the Canadians standing in the
country and they were soon found scattered from Pem-
bina on the Red River of the North to Astoria (1813)
at the mouth of the Columbia.

2. Bishop Provencher at St. Boniface.

Meanwhile no priest had been in the Northwest
country since Canada had passed under the dominion of
England. In 1818 (the year before Abbé Blanchet's
ordination) Msgr. Plessis, Bishop of Quebec, in response to petitions from the Catholic settlers in the
Red River country drawn up at the suggestion of the
Earl of Selkirk, sent two missionaries to instruct or
revive the faith among his neglected spiritual children
of the upper country. These were Abbé Joseph Norbert
Provencher, who was appointed Vicar General and
chief of the mission, and the Abbé Dumoulin, his assistant. The Abbé Provencher fixed his residence at

what is now St. Boniface, Manitoba. Four years later he was elevated to the episcopate with the title Bishop of Juliopolis *in partibus,* the auxiliary of the Bishop of Quebec and Vicar Apostolic for the District of the Northwest. With this explanation we are in a position to understand the events which led to the establishment of the Oregon mission.

3. The Willamette Settlement Requests Missionaries.

The arrival of missionaries and later of a bishop had produced among the Canadians and half-breeds and Indians of the upper country a sensation which was soon communicated to the remotest posts of the fur companies. Just at this time occurred a cessation of hostilities between the rival fur-trading companies and their union under the title of the Honorable Hudson's Bay Company, with Dr. John McLoughlin in charge of the forts in the Oregon Country. It was under McLoughlin's direction that a number of the Canadian employes of the Company whose term of office had expired were supplied with provisions and farming implements to enable them to settle in the Willamette Valley on what has since been known as French Prairie. (Chapter IV, par. 3.) This was the first agricultural settlement in the present State of Oregon, and became the nucleus of the large and prosperous Catholic settlement of St. Paul. Thus even the Canadians in distant Oregon heard the good news and longed for the coming of missionaries among them to re-animate their faith and reconcile themselves, their Indian wives and their children to the Church. Their desires found expression in petitions[1] which they drew up on July 3, 1834, and again on February 23, 1835, at the suggestion of Dr. McLoughlin. These petitions were directed to Msgr. Provencher and recited their sad spiritual conditions and begged that priests might be sent to reside with them on the banks of the Willamette. The Hudson's Bay Company would provide transportation and the Canadian settlers agreed to support the missionaries. Msgr. Provencher in answer to these petitions wrote a pastoral to his spiritual children on the Willamette and forwarded it to them through Dr. McLoughlin. The Bishop tells them that he has no priests at Red River whom he can send, but that he is on the point of starting for Canada and Europe, where he will make

---

1. The Rev. Gilbert J. Garraghan, S. J. in his *The Jesuits of the Middle United States* (New York, 1938) says (Vol. II, 236): "The Diocese of St. Louis from its erection in 1826 until 1843 not only reached as far as the Rocky Mountains but passed in some vague way, at least beyond the Continental Divide, into what was generally known as the Oregon Country.... As early as 1811 or 1812, a group of Canadian trappers and traders, ... were settled in the lower Columbia basin. They were the pioneer Catholics of that region and as early as 1821, a petition for spiritual aid on their behalf was forwarded thence to Father Rosati, vicar general of upper Louisiana. When the vicar general was so short-handed for help that parishes in the neighborhood of St. Louis could not be adequately cared for, it was impossible for him to meet the wishes of the handful of Oregon Catholics by providing them with a pastor. Ten years later, in 1831, an incident occurred that again turned the attention of Rosati, now become Bishop of St. Louis, to the spiritual needs of distant Oregon."

every effort to secure missionaries for them and for the
Indian tribes about them. He exhorts them in the
meantime to deserve by their good behavior that God
will bless his undertaking. At the same time Msgr.
Provencher wrote to Msgr. Joseph Signay, Bishop of
Quebec, concerning the expressed wish of the Catholics
of Oregon for missionaries. On the return of Bishop
Provencher from Europe it was decided to send two
priests to the new field and he at once entered into
correspondence with Governor Simpson, of the Hudson's Bay Company in London, for their transportation.

4. Mission Encouraged North of the Columbia.

The Oregon question had come to be a critical issue
between the American and English governments at this
time (1837), and the officers of the Hudson's Bay
Company in London objected to the establishment of
a mission in the Willamette Valley which, lying south
of the Columbia River, was in disputed territory. Governor Simpson suggested that the mission be established
north of the Columbia and Msgr. Provencher acquiesced
in the suggestion. A letter of Governor Simpson to
the Bishop of Quebec under date of London, February
17, 1838, sums up the correspondence:

"My Lord: I yesterday had the honor of receiving
a letter from the Bishop of Juliopolis, dated Red River,
13th October, 1837, wherein I am requested to com-

municate with your Lordship on the subject of sending two priests to the Columbia River for the purpose of establishing a Catholic mission in that part of the country.

"When the Bishop first mentioned this subject, his view was to form the mission on the banks of the Willamette, a river falling into the Columbia from the south. To the establishing of a mission there, the Governor and Committee in London and the Council in Hudson's Bay had a decided objection, as the sovereignty of that country is still undecided; but I last summer intimated to the Bishop that if he would establish the mission on the banks of the Cowlitz River, or on the Cowlitz Portage, falling into the Columbia from the northward, and give his assurance that the missionaries would not locate themselves on the south side of the Columbia River. . . . I should recommend the Governor and the Committee to afford a passage to the priests.

"By the letter received yesterday, already alluded to, the Bishop enters fully into my views and expresses his willingness to fall in with my suggestions. This letter I have laid before the Governor and Committee and am now instructed to intimate to your Lordship that if the priests will be ready at Lachine to embark for the interior about the 25th of April, a passage will be afforded them, and on the arrival at Fort Vancouver measures will be taken by the Company's representatives there to facilitate the establishing of the mission.

"Your Lordship's most obedient servant,

"GEO. SIMPSON."

5. Missionaries Appointed for Oregon.

In the meantime the Bishops had selected the priests who were destined to carry the light of the Gospel into the new field. The Bishop of Quebec gave the charge of the mission of Oregon to Abbé Blanchet, still where we left him, ministering to his flock at Cedars. By letters dated April 17, 1838, he was appointed Vicar General to the Bishop of Quebec with jurisdiction over the territory "which is comprised between the Rocky Mountains on the east, the Pacific Ocean on the west, the Russian possessions on the north and the territory of the United States on the south." Special caution was given him not to establish missions in the territory south of the Columbia, "the possession whereof is contested by the United States." The Abbé Modeste Demers, a young priest who had been ordained the previous year and who had been sent to the mission of the Red River of the North, was appointed assistant to the new Vicar General of Oregon. By an indult of the Holy See dated February 28, 1836, the Columbia country had been annexed to the Vicariate Apostolic of Msgr. Provencher of Red River.

6. From Montreal to Fort Vancouver.

The journey from Montreal to Fort Vancouver occupied six months. The distance from Lachine to Red River (2,100 miles) was made with canoes with occasional portages from one river or lake to another in a little more than a month. At Red River the Vicar General passed a month with Bishop Provencher and took his departure in company with the Abbé Demers in July for the Rocky Mountains, covering the distance of 2,000 miles in less than three months and reaching the summit of the Rockies (between Mounts Hooker and Brown in Alberta) on October 10. At 3 o'clock in the morning of that day the Vicar General celebrated Mass and consecrated — to quote his own words — "to their Creator these mountains and abrupt peaks whose prodigious heights ascend towards heaven to celebrate the praise of the Almighty." On the following Sunday the caravan arrived at Big Bend on the banks of the Columbia, and the Holy Sacrifice was offered for the first time in the Oregon Country, Abbé Demers being celebrant.

The remainder of the journey was made in light boats on the Columbia. Convenient stops were made at Forts Colville, Okanogan and Walla Walla (now Wallula). At this last post the missionaries were visited by the Walla Walla and Cayuse Indians, among whom Dr. Whitman, of the "Whitman-Saved-Oregon" myth fame, was zealously working at the Wailatpu mission. At Fort Walla Walla their visit was made pleasant by meeting with a Catholic gentleman in the person of the commandant, Mr. Pambrun. The meeting with the Cayuse Indians at this place led to closer relations in subsequent visits of Father Demers to the Fort and a growing estrangement between the Catholic and Protestant missionary forces. From Fort Walla Walla, their flotilla set out for Fort Vancouver and, after a week of slow and tedious descent of the Columbia, arrived at their destination on Saturday, November 24, 1838. They were greeted by James Douglas, who was Chief Factor and Governor of the Hudson's Bay Company west of the Rocky Mountains, in the absence of Dr. John McLoughlin on a visit to Canada and England. They had arrived at the scene of their future labors. On this date, therefore, begins the history of the Catholic Church in the Pacific Northwest.

No sooner had the missionaries reached the Fort than they were waited on by Joseph Gervais, Etienne Lucier and Pierre Beleque, a delegation representing the Canadians of the Willamette Valley. The settlers of French Prairie, on hearing that the missionaries were coming, left their homes in a body and came to Vancouver to greet them. A delay in the arrival of the Vicar General's party, however, obliged nearly all to return disappointed, leaving only three to represent them and offer to the missionaries their grateful welcome.

7. First Mass at Fort Vancouver.

The day following their arrival being Sunday, preparations were made in the school house at the Fort for the celebration of High Mass by the Vicar General. It was the first time that many of the Canadians present had been privileged to assist at the Holy Sacrifice for ten, fifteen or even twenty years. Tears came into their eyes as they reflected on the blessings which would be brought to themselves, their wives and children by the instructions and ministrations of the priests who had come among them. The employes of the Hudson's Bay Company, in active service at the twenty-eight forts for fur-trade, were for the most part Catholic; besides these were four Canadian families settled in Cowlitz, and twenty-six families in the Willamette Valley. No flattering picture of the conditions confronting him is drawn by the future Archbishop. He writes: "Many of the servants and settlers had forgotten their prayers and the religious principles they had received in their youth. The women they had taken for their wives were pagans, or baptized without sufficient knowledge. Their children were raised in ignorance. One may well imagine that in many places disorders, rudeness of morals and indecency of practices answered to that state of ignorance." (*Historical Sketches,* Ed., Bagley, p. 53.)

CHAPTER FOUR

LAYING THE FOUNDATIONS

An Extended Mission. — The Cowlitz Settlement
Visited. — The First House of Worship in Oregon. —
The Catholic Ladder. — Father Demers at Fort Nes-
qually. — Antagonism Between Rival Missionaries. —
Mission Permitted South of the Columbia. — Astoria
and Whidbey Island

1. An Extended Mission.

Father Blanchet began his work by opening at Fort
Vancouver for the Catholics of the place a mission
which lasted with very little interruption from the end
of November, 1838, to the middle of April of the next
year. A census taken at the time showed seventy-six
Catholics at the Fort, including a number of Catholic
Iroquois, as well as the Canadian employes. During
the mission especial attention was paid to the Indians.
In the morning and evening Father Demers, who had
mastered the Chinook jargon, taught them the prayers
he had translated for them, and in the afternoon about
one hundred women and children gathered for instruction preparatory to baptism. While Father Demers was
instructing the Indians, the Vicar General taught the
Canadians, giving instructions both in French and English, so that some of those who were more apt were

soon able to assist in teaching the prayers and catechism to others. The teaching of Gregorian chant was a matter of special pride with the Vicar General, and he always mentions with satisfaction the solemn chanting of the services by the savages in his various missions.

2. The Cowlitz Settlement Visited.

According to the agreement already mentioned, between Msgr. Provencher and Sir George Simpson, the Catholic mission was to be established on the Cowlitz River, as the settlement on the Willamette (then called Wallamet) was in disputed territory. Accordingly, the Vicar General left Vancouver on December 12, in a canoe paddled by four Indians, and arrived at the Cowlitz settlement on Sunday, December 16. He celebrated Mass in the house of one of the Canadian settlers, Mr. Simon Plamondon. He chose for the mission six hundred and forty acres of clear prairie land and left his servant to square the timbers for a house and barn and to make rails for fences. On leaving, he appointed one of the farmers, Mr. Fagnant, to teach the prayers and catechism to the women and children until the next visit of the missionaries.

3. The First House of Worship in Oregon.

The fact that no mission was to be established south of the Columbia did not deter the Vicar General from attending to the spiritual wants of the settlers who had first sent the Macedonian cry to the bishops of Canada. On his return from Cowlitz he spent his first Christmas in the West at Fort Vancouver, celebrating midnight Mass with great solemnity — a custom which he never failed to observe. On January 3, 1839, he set out for the settlement in the Willamette Valley a few miles above Champoeg, near the present town of St. Paul. The history of this settlement is related by Archbishop Blanchet as follows:

"There remained in the country three Canadians, remnants of the old expeditions of Hunt and Astor, viz., Etienne Lucier, one of the former, and Joseph Gervais and Louis Labonte of the latter. Etienne Lucier being tired of living a wandering life, began in 1829 to cultivate the land near Fort Vancouver, and getting dissatisfied with his first choice, left it in 1830, and removing to the Willamette Valley, settled a few miles above Champoeg, then called by the Canadians 'Campement de Sable.' Following his example, the two others followed him in 1831 and settled some distance south of him, one on the right, and the other on the left side of the river. Some old servants of the Hudson's Bay Company, being discharged from further service, went over to them and increased their number. The good and generous Dr. McLoughlin encouraged the colony and helped it all in his power." (*Historical Sketches,* p. 62.) This was the community which had petitioned Msgr. Provencher for a spiritual guide. When the Vicar General arrived at Champoeg he was provided with a mount and rode to the church, which stood at a distance of four miles. The church, the first erected in Oregon, a log structure, thirty by seventy feet, had been built in 1836, having been undertaken as soon as the settlers had received Msgr. Provencher's pastoral promising them missionaries and exhorting them to the faithful practice of their religion. Father Blanchet took possession of a small room behind the altar and spent the afternoon in receiving visits from the people, whose ardent wishes had that day been realized.

The following day, January 6, being Sunday and the feast of the Epiphany, the church, the first in the Pacific Northwest, was blessed under the patronage of the Apostle St. Paul, and Holy Mass, for the first time in the present State of Oregon, was celebrated in the presence of the Canadians, their wives and children. For four weeks the Vicar General conducted a mission among them, instructing all, baptizing the women and children and blessing the marriages. Before leaving he took possession of a section of land around the church, because both he and the settlers had every confidence that Dr. McLoughlin would secure permission for the establishment of a permanent mission on the Willamette.

4. The Catholic Ladder.

After a few weeks at Fort Vancouver, the Vicar General set out again for Cowlitz and opened a mission there in the house of Mr. Plamondon on Passion Sunday, March 17, 1839. The mission continued until Easter, the ceremonies of Holy Week making a deep impression upon all who attended. A device called "The Catholic Ladder," adopted by Father Blanchet on the occasion of this mission, was to exert a wide influence in all the early Catholic missionary work among the Indians in Oregon. The news of the arrival of the missionary at Cowlitz caused numerous delegations of Indians to come from remote distances in order to see and hear the black-gown. Among these was one from an Indian tribe on Whidbey Island, Puget Sound, 150 miles from the Cowlitz mission. After a journey of two days in canoes to Fort Nesqually and an arduous march of three days on foot, across streams and rivers and by an exceedingly rough trail, they reached Cowlitz with bleeding feet, and famished. When they were refreshed, the missionary began to explain to them the teachings of the Christian religion. In his *Historical Sketches* Archbishop Blanchet gives the following account of the matter:

"The great difficulty was to give them an idea of religion so plain and simple as to command their attention . . . and which they would carry back with them to their tribes. In looking for a plan the Vicar General imagined that by representing on a square stick the forty centuries before Christ by forty marks; the thirty-three years of our Lord by thirty-three points followed by a cross; and the eighteen centuries and thirty-nine years since, by eighteen marks and thirty-nine points, his design would be pretty well answered, giving him a chance to show the beginning of the world, the creation, the fall of the angels, of Adam, the promise of a Saviour, the time of His birth, and His death upon the cross as well as the mission of the Apostles. The plan was a great success. After eight days of explanation the chief and his companions became masters of the subject . . . and started for home well satisfied with a square rule thus marked." (Page 69.)

The same scheme was soon after worked out on a chart, at first simply, but later in a very elaborate manner. A copy of this chart in its final form, as copyrighted by Archbishop Blanchet in 1859, measures five feet in length and two and a half feet in width. It is a veritable pictorial compendium of Biblical and Church history. The use of the Catholic Ladder spread very rapidly, and a copy of the chart was to be found in every Indian camp visited by a Catholic missionary. In the absence of the priest, the Indian chiefs took great pride in expounding the "Ladder" to their people. Father De Smet praised it very highly, and the view taken of it by the Protestant missionaries may be seen from the fact that they tried to counteract its influence by a "Protestant Ladder" in which the history of the Catholic Church was traced as the broad way that leads to perdition. It is certain that this concrete and pictorial presentation of religion was much better suited to the capabilities of the savage than the abstract doctrinal methods employed by the Protestant missionaries, and it achieved more success.

5. Father Demers at Fort Nesqually.

While he was conducting the mission at Cowlitz, the Vicar General was informed that the Methodists were about to open an establishment among the Indians at Fort Nesqually. He immediately dispatched Father Demers thither, feeling that it would be easier to gain the attention of the savages before they had been exposed to hostile teachers. A ten days' mission by Father Demers resulted in gaining the good will of the Indians, in bringing back to the practice of their religion the Canadian employes of the Fort and in the conversion of Mrs. Kitson, the wife of the commandant[1] at Fort Nesqually, who thereafter acted as interpreter. Father Demers made arrangements to build a chapel at Fort Nesqually and hastened back to Fort Vancouver to take passage on one of the barges of the

---

1. Mr. Kitson was received into the Church the following year.

Hudson's Bay Company for the Upper Columbia settlements. The summer months of 1839 found him giving missions at Forts Colville, Okanogan and Walla Walla, to the great spiritual benefit of both the savages and the Canadians. In October Father Demers was back again at the Cowlitz. From a letter written at this time we get the interesting information that on the 14th of October he blessed a fifty-pound bell and after having it placed in position, rang the Angelus — the first time in the Oregon Country.[2]

6. Antagonism Between Rival Missionaries.

Meanwhile the Vicar General revisited the settlement on the Willamette and later conducted a successful mission at Fort Nesqually. At the former place no little excitement was caused by the antagonism of the rival missionaries. A number of marriages and baptisms were performed by Father Blanchet in cases where the Methodist ministers had already officiated. The ministers had also established a temperance society and gathered in a number of Catholics — which would doubtless have been good for them had it not been made a means of perverting their faith. When the Catholic mission was established, the Catholics with-

2. This was in the present State of Washington. The Vicar General had an eighty-pound bell set in place and blessed at St. Paul two days before Christmas, 1839. This was the first bell to peal forth the Angelus in the present State of Oregon.

drew from the society, much to the chagrin of the opposing missionaries. To disaffect the minds of people towards the Catholic mission, a copy of the vile "disclosures" of Maria Monk was circulated in the community. When the true character of the book was made known, its circulation produced an effect contrary to that intended, and it was quietly withdrawn.

7. Mission Permitted South of the Columbia.

The first year of missionary life in Oregon closed auspiciously with notice from the Hudson's Bay Company that the Governor and Committee had reconsidered their objection to the establishment of a Catholic mission on the south side of the Columbia and that the missionaries were at liberty to make such a foundation on the Willamette. The news was conveyed to the Vicar General by acting Governor James Douglas in the absence of Dr. McLoughlin, who was in Europe. The change of attitude on the part of the Company was effected by the representations of Dr. McLoughlin while in London. McLoughlin returned to Fort Vancouver in the fall of 1839 and paid a visit to the settlement on the Willamette, where he was greeted as a father. This was the occasion of his first meeting with the future Archbishop.

8. Astoria and Whidbey Island.

During the year 1840, our missionaries laid the foundation of two important establishments, the one at Astoria at the mouth of the Columbia, the other at Whidbey Island on Puget Sound. Father Demers reached Astoria on May 21 and on the following day pitched his tent among the Chinook Indians. At the time of his arrival, the ship, Lausanne, had just crossed the Columbia bar with the "great reinforcement" for the Methodist mission on the Willamette. Father Demers "with a little bell in one hand and a 'Catholic Ladder' in the other continued his mission for three weeks, instructing the adults, baptizing the children and doing much good." Meanwhile the Vicar General had made his way by canoe from Fort Nesqually to Whidbey Island on Puget Sound, where he erected a massive cross (whence Commodore Wilkes called it Cross Island) and gathered the savages about him for daily instruction.

CHAPTER FIVE

THE MISSIONARIES

Arrival of the Protestant Missionaries. — McLoughlin's Kindness to the Methodists. — "The Great Reinforcement." — Catholic Services at Fort Vancouver.
— Conversion of McLoughlin

I. Arrival of the Protestant Missionaries.

McLoughlin's relations with the early missionaries
form an interesting·chapter in the events of this period.
The first missionaries to arrive were the Methodist ministers, Rev. Jason Lee and his nephew, Rev. Daniel Lee.
They came with Wyeth's second expedition in 1834.
The following year, Rev. Samuel Parker, a Presbyterian
minister, arrived at Fort Vancouver. Parker returned
to the East in 1837, and published a book, entitled,
*Journal of an Exploring Tour Beyond the Rocky Moun-
tains,* in which he speaks of his reception at the Fort
in the following terms: "Dr. J. McLoughlin, a chief
factor and superintendent of this fort and of the business of the company west of the Rocky Mountains, received me with many expressions of kindness, and invited me to make his residence my home for the winter,
and as long as it would suit my convenience." In the
same work, under date of Monday, May 11, 1836, he
says: "Having made arrangements to leave this place

40

on the 14th, I called upon the chief clerk for my bill.
He said the Company had made no bill against me,
but felt a pleasure in gratuitously conferring all they
have done for the benefit of the object in which I am engaged." In 1836, two men representing the American
Board Missions, who acquired much notoriety in early
Oregon history, namely, Dr. Marcus Whitman and Rev.
H. H. Spalding, came to Vancouver. They were destitute when they arrived at the Fort. Dr. McLoughlin,
with his usual kindness, furnished them with everything
they needed and permitted Mrs. Whitman and Mrs.
Spalding to make their home at the Fort for several
months while the men were establishing the Mission.
Marcus Whitman is the hero whose famous mid-winter
ride has been recited in prose and verse. (See Chapter
XV for a discussion of the Whitman Legend.)

2. McLoughlin's Kindness to the Methodists.

The Methodist missionaries, as has been said, came
in the year 1834. They were received by McLoughlin
with his usual open-handed hospitality and were assisted in establishing their Mission, being treated, as
Jason Lee says in his diary under date of September 29,
1834, "with the utmost politeness, attention and liber-
ality." At the invitation of Dr. McLoughlin, Jason Lee
preached at the Fort. In March, 1836, the officers at
the Fort made up a purse of more than a hundred dollars which they presented to Lee for the Mission. In

fact, from their inception and for some years after, the success of all the missions, whether Methodist or Presbyterian, was due to the generosity of McLoughlin. This is frankly admitted by Rev. Gustavus Hines, the Methodist author of the *Missionary History of the Pacific Northwest*. In 1837 the Methodist mission was increased by the arrival at Vancouver of a party including Anna Maria Pittman, who soon became the wife of Jason Lee. Early in 1838 Lee went East on business for the Mission. He had been gone three months when his young wife died. With the fine thoughtfulness and simplicity that characterized him, Dr. McLoughlin dispatched a messenger as far as Westport, Missouri, to bear the news to Jason Lee. In view of these acts of kindness, the subsequent conduct of the members of the Mission towards Dr. McLoughlin can be read only with astonishment. (See Chapter XII.)

3. "The Great Reinforcement."

While Jason Lee was in the East on the occasion just mentioned, he induced the Missionary Board to raise $42,000 to send a large party of missionaries with plentiful provisions to Oregon on the ship Lausanne. The party that reached Vancouver in 1840 on the Lausanne is known in Methodist annals as the "great reinforcement." Among the number were Rev. Alvin Waller and George Abernethy, who was to be steward of the Mission, and who afterwards held the position of

Governor during the time of the Provisional Government of Oregon. These men were to cause McLoughlin much trouble. When the Lausanne arrived McLoughlin sent fresh provisions to the members of the "great reinforcement" and provided for them at the Fort. "Why this large addition to the Oregon Mission and these quantities of supplies were sent and this great expense incurred," says Mr. Holman, "has never been satisfactorily explained. The Methodist Oregon Mission was then, so far as converting the Indians, a failure." After 1843 the station lost much of its character as a mission and became a trading post.

4. Catholic Services at Fort Vancouver.

Meanwhile, as already narrated, the Catholic missionaries came on the scene and Father Blanchet quite naturally became intimately acquainted with Dr. McLoughlin. During the years immediately following 1838 the two became close friends. It was due to the influence of Father Blanchet that Dr. McLoughlin was brought to investigate the claims of the Catholic Church. The only account we possess of the circumstances surrounding the conversion of Dr. McLoughlin is that given by Archbishop Blanchet in his *Historical Sketches of the Catholic Church in Oregon,* published by the Catholic Sentinel Press in 1878. Under the caption, "The Remarkable Conversion of Dr. John McLoughlin," we read:

"It is but just to make special mention of the important services which Dr. John McLoughlin — though not a Catholic — has rendered to the French Canadians and their families, during the fourteen years he was Governor at Fort Vancouver. He it was who read to them the prayers on Sunday. Besides the English school kept for the children of the bourgeois, he had a separate one maintained at his own expense, in which prayers and catechism were taught in French to the Catholic women and children on Sundays and week days by his order.[1] He also encouraged the chant of the canticles, in which he was assisted by his wife and daughter, who took much pleasure in this exercise. He visited and examined his school once a week, which was already formed of several good scholars, who soon learned to read French and became of great help to the priest. He it was who saved the Catholics of the Fort and their children from the dangers of perversion, and who, finding the log church the Canadians had built a few miles below Fairfield in 1836, not properly located, ordered it to be removed and rebuilt on a large prairie, its present beautiful site.

5. Conversion of McLoughlin.

"To that excellent man was our holy religion indebted for whatever morality the missionaries found at Vancouver as well as for the welfare and temporal ad-

---

1. The first schools in the Pacific Northwest.

vantages the settlers of the Cowlitz and Willamette Valleys enjoyed at that time. At the time the two missionaries arrived Dr. McLoughlin was absent, but was expected to return in the following September. The good work of that upright man deserved a reward; he received it by being brought to the true Church in the following manner: When he was once on a visit to Fort Nesqually, *The End of Controversy,* by Dr. Milner, fell into his hands. He read it with avidity and was overcome and converted by it at once. On his return to Fort Vancouver he made his abjuration and profession of Faith at the hands of the Vicar General, on November 18, 1842. He made his confession, had his marriage blessed on the same day, and prepared himself for his First Communion by fasting during the four weeks of Advent, which he passed on his claim at the Willamette Falls, now called Oregon City, in having the place surveyed into blocks and lots. Being thus prepared, he made his First Communion at Fort Vancouver at midnight Mass on Christmas, with a large number of faithful women and servants of the Hudson's Bay Company. The little chapel was then full of white people and Indians; it was beautifully decorated and brilliantly illuminated; the plain chant was grave; the chant of the canticles of Noel in French and Chinook jargon, alternately by two choirs of men and women, was impressive, as well as was the holy ceremony around the altar; in a word, it was captivating and elevating to the minds of the faithful commemorating the great day of the birth of our Saviour. From the time of his conversion till his death, Dr. McLoughlin showed himself a true and practical Christian and a worthy member of Holy Church; never missing the divine services of Mass and Vespers on Sunday and holydays; going to the holy table nearly monthly and preaching strongly by word and example. On going to church each Sunday he was often accompanied by some Protestant friends; one of them inviting him to go and assist at the services of their church, he answered him: 'No, sir, I go to the Church that teaches truth, but not to a Church that teaches error.' On hearing of this great man the Holy Father, Pope Gregory XVI, sent him the insignia of the Knights of the Distinguished Order of St. Gregory, which Archbishop Blanchet delivered to him on his return from Europe in August, 1847."[1]

---

1. This decoration was established by Pope Gregory XVI. Was McLoughlin perhaps the first on this side of the Atlantic to receive this honor?

CHAPTER SIX

THE AMERICAN IMMIGRATION

1. The Outlook in 1842.

At the time of his conversion McLoughlin's fortunes and powers were at their zenith; his prospects were golden. During the years of his administration at Fort Vancouver he had built up the business of his Company to enormous proportions. The Indians were peaceful and obedient and he commanded the respect as well as the obedience of the officers and employes of the Company. His salary reached, what was for those times, the considerable sum of several thousand dollars annually. He had completed his fifty-eighth year with the physical and mental powers of the very prime of manhood. Joining the Catholic Church at this time was, humanly speaking, most ill-advised. To the prejudice against McLoughlin as a British subject before and during the "54-40 or fight" campaign of Polk in 1844, was added the prejudice against him as a Catholic, which, as Mr. Holman remarks, was intensified locally in Oregon by "a partial success of the Roman Catholic missionaries with the Indians, where the Protestants had failed." Then, there was also McLoughlin's land claim at Oregon City, which was coveted by members of the Methodist Mission, and of which we shall have occasion to speak later on. The ten years following the conversion of McLoughlin were to witness important developments in the Oregon Country.

2. American Immigration Begins.

Beginning with 1842, a tide of immigration set towards Oregon from the Eastern States. Of the one hundred and twenty-five persons who came in 1842, a part only remained in Oregon. On their arrival they were assisted very generously by Dr. McLoughlin and, when nearly half of their number set out for California a few months later, they were furnished by him with supplies, with the understanding that they would repay the Hudson's Bay Company's agent, at Yerba Buena (now San Francisco).

The first great influx of home-builders came in 1843. The company, consisting of nearly nine hundred persons, set out from Independence, Mo., on their long and tedious journey across the plains and mountains. They were led by Hon. Peter H. Burnett, who became the first Governor of California, and J. W. Nesmith, afterwards United States Senator from Oregon. On reaching the Columbia River they followed its course.

Their greatest difficulty was in getting from the upper to the lower Cascades. As the rafts could not be taken over the rapids, it was necessary to cut a trail around the Cascades. Meanwhile the rains set in. The condition of the immigrants became desperate. They had not anticipated such hardships and were ill prepared for them. Few had sufficient food or clothing, and many were absolutely destitute. Dr. Loughlin came to their relief. He furnished boats to carry them from the Cascades to Vancouver. He sold supplies to those who were able to pay and gave credit without collateral to all who were in want. By his orders the sick were nursed and cared for in the Company's hospital at the Fort.

3. Indian Massacre Averted.

While the immigrants were following the course of the Columbia River, The Dalles Indians plotted to massacre the entire party. One may conjecture what would have been the result of such a catastrophe. It might have prevented for some years the development of the Oregon Country by the Americans, and this is precisely what the Hudson's Bay Company would have desired. They wished to prevent the settlement of the country, so as to keep it a rich field for their exploitation, a wild country for wild animals. To carry out the wishes of his Company, Dr. McLoughlin need only have permitted events to take their course. The Indians would have discouraged immigration, and the Oregon Country might have been saved to Great Britain and the Hudson's Bay Company for years to come. But McLoughlin put aside the interests of company and country to protect the higher interests of humanity. We learn from his own pen how the massacre was averted. In a document now in the possession of the Oregon Historical Association he says:

"In 1843, about 800 immigrants arrived from the States. I saw by the look of the Indians that they were excited, and I watched them. As the first stragglers were arriving at Vancouver in canoes, and I was standing on the bank, nearer the water there was a group of ten or twelve Indians. One of them bawled out to his companions, 'It is good for us to kill these Bostons (Americans).' Struck with the excitement I had seen in the countenances of the Indians since they had heard the report of the immigration coming, I felt certain they were inclined to mischief, and that he spoke thus loud as a feeler to sound me, and to take their measures accordingly. I immediately rushed on them with my cane, calling out at the same time, 'Who is the dog that says it is a good thing to kill the Bostons?' The fellow trembling, excused himself, 'I spoke without meaning harm, but The Dalles Indians say so.' 'Well,' said I, 'The Dalles Indians are dogs for saying so and you also,' and left them. I had done enough to convince them I would not allow them to do wrong to the immigrants with impunity. . . . I immediately formed my plan and kept my knowledge of the horrid designs of the Indians secret, as I felt certain that if the Americans knew it, these men acting independently of each other would be at once for fighting, which would lead to their total destruction, and I sent two boats with provisions to meet them; sent provisions to Mr. Burnett . . . being confident that the fright I had given the Indians who said it was a good thing to kill the Bostons, was known at The Dalles before our boats were there, and that the presence of the Hudson's Bay Company people, and the assistance they afforded the immigrants, would deter the Indians from doing any wrong, and I am happy to be able to say that I entirely succeeded."

4. McLoughlin Provides Seed Wheat.

When the immigrants arrived at their destination their trials did not cease. They had come in the fall of the year and were without provisions. The problem was to provide for their needs until the next harvest, if, indeed, they should have a harvest. Again McLoughlin came to their relief without solicitation. He furnished the necessary supplies, gave credit, supplied food and clothing and loaned the settlers seed wheat and farm implements. All this, it will be remembered, was strictly against the regulations and policy of the Hudson's Bay Company. In referring to the treatment accorded to the immigrants, Mr. Burnett, who led the party, wrote in his journal of travels: "The kindness of Dr. McLoughlin to this emigration has been very great. He furnished them with goods and provisions on credit, and such as were sick were sent to the hospital free of expense, where they had the strict and careful attendance of Dr. Barclay, a skilful physician. . . . Had it not been for the kindness of this excellent man (McLoughlin) many of us would have suffered greatly." Much more could be quoted from immigrants of 1843 to the same effect.

5. The Immigrants of 1844 Receive Aid.

The following year witnessed an increased immigration. About fourteen hundred persons formed the company. A large part of their goods and provisions were lost in the long journey. Again Dr. McLoughlin came to the rescue. John Minto, one of the pioneers of 1844, states that the immigrants of that year descended the Columbia River in boats furnished from the fort; the hungry were fed and the sick cared for and nursed in the hospital. Another pioneer of 1844, Joseph Watt, gives the following account in his *Recollections of Dr. John McLoughlin:* "We had eaten the last of our provisions at our last camp, and were told by Hess (whom McLoughlin had sent with a bateau to bring the party down the Columbia) that we could get plenty at the fort, with or without money; that the old Doctor never turned people away hungry. This made us feel quite comfortable, for there was not a dollar among us. . . . We soon found the Doctor in a small room he called his office. . . . We then made known to him our wants. We were all out of provisions." McLoughlin offered to supply provisions at the fort for their immediate necessity. "Several of our party broke in, saying: 'Doctor, I have no money to pay, and I don't know when or how I can pay you.' 'Tut, tut, never mind that; you can't suffer,' said the Doctor. He then commenced at the head man saying, 'Your name, if you please; how many in the family, and what do you desire?' Upon receiving an answer, the Doctor wrote an order, directing him where to go and have it filled; then called up the next man, and so on until we were all supplied. . . . Such was the case with every boat-load, and all those who came by land down the train. . . . "

6. Provisions Furnished to 3,000 Immigrants in 1845.

In 1845, about three thousand people came to Oregon. There was quite as much destitution among the new arrivals as there had been during the preceding year. Mrs. Perry, who lived at St. Helen's, Oregon, was one of the immigrants of 1845. She informed the present writer that the company became destitute of provisions long before they reached Oregon. Fortunately, in those days the countless buffaloes that ranged the plains furnished means of sustenance. Mrs. Perry continued: "No food ever tasted better than the buffalo meat dried in the dust as it hung on strings on the side of the immigrant wagon. When the lower Cascades were reached we were met by a bateau sent by Dr. McLoughlin with provisions for the party. Each family was supplied with flour enough for one baking." Another pioneer of 1845, who has left an account of the arrival of the party in Oregon, was Stephen Staats. "On our arrival (at Oregon City)," said Mr. Staats, in his address before the Oregon Pioneer Association in 1877, "those of us in advance were kindly and hospitably received by old Dr. McLoughlin. He immediately furnished us with provisions, without money and without price." The immigration of 1845 is the last with which we are concerned here. Before the arrival of the immigrants the following year, McLoughlin's resignation from the Hudson's Bay Company had taken effect.

7. Two Important Considerations.

In forming any adequate estimate of the assistance rendered by McLoughlin to the early immigrants, two facts must be borne in mind, namely, that his action was in direct opposition to the policy of his Company, and that while he was performing these works of kindness he was aware that members of the Methodist Mission were trying to rob him of his extensive land claim at Oregon City. Of this injustice we shall speak presently. In answer to the question whether the secular department of the Methodist Mission assisted the early immigrants in a way similar to what was done by Dr. McLoughlin, Mr. Holman writes (page 89): "If so, I have found no trace nor record of it. Undoubtedly Methodist missionaries, individually, did many kindly acts to destitute immigrants. Had Dr. McLoughlin acted with the supineness of the Methodist Mission towards the immigrants of 1843, 1844 and 1845, and especially that of 1843, the consequences would have been terrible."

8. McLoughlin's Resignation.

The Hudson's Bay Company, as has been said, was opposed to the humanitarianism displayed by Dr. McLoughlin. In 1845 Capt. Warre and Lieut. Vavasour, of the British army, were sent to Oregon to make a military report of the condition of the country. They remained in the neighborhood of Vancouver for some time and were present when McLoughlin succored the American immigrants of 1845. They also learned how he had given assistance to the settlers of preceding years, and reported adversely on his conduct. As regards the claims of England, it will be remembered that the Oregon Country during McLoughlin's administration was in a condition of Joint Occupancy as provided by the Convention of 1818 between our country and Great Britain. Consequently American citizens in the Oregon Country had precisely the same rights as had British subjects. The Hudson's Bay Comany had, indeed, a monopoly of the fur trade from the British government, but with the express stipulation that American traders should not be interfered with. The special advantages of the Company had enabled it to maintain a practical monopoly in Oregon for a quarter of a century, and it naturally enough came to regard the Americans as trespassing on its private reserves. Dr. McLoughlin answered the charge in a dignified manner. He pointed out that his action was for the best interests of the Company; he had neither the right nor the power to drive the Americans out of the territory; consequently he did his best to prevent them from becoming idle and dangerous to the Company. He admitted giving assistance to the early immigrants, saving the lives and property of the sick and destitute, and making it possible for the settlers to raise a crop for themselves and for the next year's immigrants, instead of permitting them to become dependent on the Company for support. "If we had not done this," said he, "Vancouver would have been destroyed and the world would have judged us treated as our inhuman conduct deserved; every officer of the Company, from the Governor down, would have been covered with obloquy, the Company's business in this department would have been ruined, and the trouble which would have arisen in consequence would have probably involved the British and American nations in war. If I have been the means, by my measures, of arresting any of these evils, I shall be amply repaid by the approbation of my conscience."

Sir George Simpson, who was Governor-in-Chief of the Hudson's Bay Company, criticized McLoughlin severely for assisting the Americans. The correspondence became very bitter. McLoughlin declared that no person possessed of common humanity could do otherwise than he had done. This brought back a command from Simpson to render no further aid to the immigrants. The tension between the Governor and the Chief Factor was further accentuated by bitter recriminations occasioned by the murder of McLoughlin's son John in 1842. McLoughlin charged Simpson with responsibility for the murder. Moreover McLoughlin, with the motive of safeguarding the Company's interests, purchased the Company's mills at Oregon City, and found himself in the ambiguous position of being engaged in private business although still acting as Chief Factor. As a result of Governor Simpson's attitude in all these matters McLoughlin was led to submit his resignation. That was in 1845. Twelve months had to elapse before the resignation became effective. In 1846 he retired to Oregon City to pass his remaining days on the land claim he had taken up as early as 1829. He looked forward to a peaceful and happy old age in his new home. But he was destined to be sadly disappointed in his hopes.

REV. P. J. DeSmet, S. J.

CHAPTER SEVEN

THE MACEDONIAN CRY

Canadian Fur Traders Spread the Faith. — Iroquois Indians Carry Catholic Faith. — Deputation Goes to St. Louis. — Young Ignace Meets DeSmet. — Indian Missions Confided to Jesuits. — DeSmet Sets Out for Oregon. — In the Land of the Shoshones. — Fervor of the Flatheads. — At the Continental Divide. — The White Man's Book of Heaven

1. Canadian Fur-Traders Spread the Faith.

We have learned how the first tidings of the Catholic faith reached the Oregon Indians through the trappers of the various fur-trading companies who had learned their religion from the pioneer missionaries of Quebec and Montreal. Canadian voyageurs formed a large element in the expeditions of Lewis and Clark in 1805 and of John Jacob Astor in 1811. This latter expedition especially, which resulted in establishing at the mouth of the Columbia the first American settlement in Oregon, the present flourishing city of Astoria, was accompanied by a number of Catholic Canadians, who became the first settlers in the Willamette Valley. The piety of these voyageurs may be seen in the rather unusual fact that the early missionaries on their arrival found a church already erected.

2. Iroquois Indians Carry Catholic Faith.

Another agency instrumental in bringing the faith to the Far West was the Iroquois Indians. These Indians, among whose tribe the seeds of faith had been sown at an early date by Father Jogues, were in the employ of the Hudson's Bay Company at its various forts. The trappers and Iroquois told the tribes of Oregon of the religion of the black-robes, taught them the simple prayers they remembered, inculcated the observance of Sunday and aroused among them a great desire to receive the ministrations of the black-robes. An Iroquois named Ignace became a veritable apostle to the Flatheads. Such was the effect of his teachings and example that the Flatheads, together with their neighbors, the Nez Perces, sent a deputation to St. Louis in 1831 to ask for priests.[1]

3. Deputation Goes to St. Louis.

It was to St. Louis rather than to Montreal that the Indians turned for assistance, for since the days of the

---

1. *"Bonneville,* Chap. X, mentions this band of Iroquois and also the piety of the Flatheads, and in Chap. XLV Irving not only quotes Bonneville's, but also Wyeth's testimony as to the observance by the Nez Perces of the religious (Catholic) services they had learned from the Hudson's Bay Company traders, especially Pambrun at Fort Walla Walla and from these Iroquois. Wyeth's *Journal* (published by the Oregon Historical Society) also states the same thing more fully than Irving's *Bonneville,"* p. 11. This was before any missionaries had gone to either tribe.

"Father Palladino says that somewhere between 1812 and 1820 a band of about twenty-four Iroquois from the Caughnawaga Mission near Montreal wandered into and across the Rocky Mountains as far

great travelers, Lewis and Clark, the traders had renewed their relations annually with that city. The deputation consisted of four Indians. They found Clark
still living in St. Louis. Two of the company took sick
and died after receiving baptism and the last sacraments. The return of the remaining members of the
deputation is uncertain. They had repeated the Macedonian cry, "Come over and help us." The Catholic
missionary forces were too weak to respond at once to
the appeal. But the presence of the Indians in St. Louis
from far distant Oregon on such a mission was the occasion of a movement with far-reaching results. The
incident was given publicity in the Protestant religious
press, and aroused wonderful enthusiasm and set on
foot perhaps the most remarkable missionary campaign
in the history of this country; a campaign which was
fraught with important consequences for Oregon. The
Methodists came in 1834 under the leadership of Jason
Lee (Chapter V), and Dr. Whitman with Spalding
and Gray, of the American Board Mission, arrived at
Vancouver in 1836.

---

west as the Flathead Valley in what is now Northwest Montana,
and being pleased with the country and with the Selish or Flathead
tribe, concluded to remain there and intermarry with them. The
leader of this band was Ignace La Mousse, better known among the
Indians as Big Ignace or Old Ignace. He became prominent among
the Flatheads, and being a zealous Catholic, taught them what he
could of that faith and excited among them so strong a desire for
'Black Robes' that in the spring of 1831 a deputation of two Flatheads and two Nez Perces started to St. Louis to obtain priests and
arrived there in the autumn of 1831." Marshall, Vol. 2, p. 11.

4. Young Ignace Meets DeSmet.

But to return to our Flatheads. In 1835 the Flathead chief, Insula, went to the Green River rendezvous to meet those whom he was informed were the black-gowns. Much to his disappointment he met, not the priests, but Dr. Whitman and Rev. Mr. Parker, of the American Board. On reporting his ill-success it was determined that the old Iroquois Ignace and his two sons should go in search of missionaries. They met Bishop Rosati at St. Louis, but were unsuccessful in their quest. Nothing daunted, they renewed the attempt, and a deputation under young Ignace again reached St. Louis in 1839. It was on this occasion that DeSmet comes into view for the first time. Young Ignace and his companions paused at Council Bluffs to visit the priests at St. Joseph Mission, where Father DeSmet was stationed. DeSmet gives us the following record of the meeting:

"On the 18th of September last two Catholic Iroquois came to visit us. They had been for twenty-three years among the nations called the Flatheads and Pierced Noses about a thousand Flemish leagues from where we are. I have never seen any savages so fervent in religion. By their instructions and example they have given all that nation a great desire to have themselves baptized. All that tribe strictly observe Sunday and assemble several times a week to pray and sing canticles. The sole object of these good Iroquois was to obtain a priest to come and finish what they had happily commenced. We gave them letters of recommendation for our Reverend Father Superior at St. Louis." Father DeSmet could scarcely have hoped that it should be his privilege to receive these children of the forest, who so greatly interested him, into the fold of Christ.

5. Indian Missions Confided to Jesuits.

Meanwhile certain other events occurred that affected the Oregon Indians. In 1833 the second Provincial Council of Baltimore petitioned that the Indian missions of the United States be confided to the care of the Society of Jesus. In July of the following year the Holy See acceded to the request. Hence, when the the deputation of Indians visited St. Louis and obtained from Bishop Rosati the promise of missionaries, it was to the Jesuit Fathers that the Bishop turned for volunteers. In a letter to the Father General of the Society in Rome under date of October 20, 1839, Bishop Rosati relates in detail the story of the various journeys of the Indians in search of the black-robes and gives us the following interesting account of young Ignace and his companion, Pierre Gaucher:

"At last, a third deputation of Indians arrived at St. Louis after a long voyage of three months. It is composed of two Christian Iroquois. These Indians, who talk French, have edified us by their truly exemplary conduct and interested us by their discourse. The fathers of the college have heard their confessions, and today they approached the holy table at my Mass in the Cathedral church. Afterwards I administered to them the sacrament of Confirmation; and in an allocution delivered after the ceremony, I rejoiced with them in their happiness and gave them the hope of soon having a priest."

6. DeSmet Sets Out for Oregon.

Father DeSmet, deeply impressed by the visit of young Ignace, offered to devote himself to the Indian missions. The offer was gratefully accepted by his Superior and by the Bishop, and DeSmet set out on his first trip to the Oregon country late in March, 1840. Past Westport (now Kansas City) he journeyed along the Platte River, through herds of antelope and buffalo, across the country of the Pawnees and Cheyennes to the South Pass across the Continental Divide. Here, on June 25, he passed from the waters tributary to the Missouri to those of the Colorado. "On the 30th (of June)," says Father DeSmet, "I came to the rendezvous where a band of Flatheads, who had been notified of my coming, were already waiting for me. This happened on the Green River, a tributary of the Colorado. It is the place where the beaver hunters and the savages of different nations betake themselves every year to sell their peltries and procure such things as they need." On the following Sunday, Father DeSmet assembled the Indians and trappers for divine worship. In a letter dated February 4, 1841, he writes: "On Sunday, the 5th of July, I had the consolation of celebrating the Holy Sacrifice of Mass *sub dio*. The altar was placed on an elevation, and surrounded with boughs and garlands of flowers; I addressed the congregation in French and in English and spoke also by an interpreter to the Flatheads and Snake Indians. It was a spectacle truly moving for the heart of a missionary to behold an assembly composed of so many different nations, who all assisted at our holy mysteries with great satisfaction. The Canadians sang hymns in French and Latin, and the Indians in their native tongue. It was truly a Catholic worship. This place has been called since that time, by the French Canadians, 'La Prairie de la Messe.' "

7. In the Land of the Shoshones.

DeSmet was now in the land of the Shoshone or Snake Indians. Three hundred of their warriors came into camp at full gallop. DeSmet was invited to a council of some thirty of the principal chiefs. "I explained to them," he writes, "the Christian doctrines in a compendious manner. They were all very attentive; they then deliberated among themselves for about half an hour and one of the chiefs, addressing me in the name of the others, said: 'Black-gown, the words of thy mouth have found their way to our hearts; they will never be forgotten.' I advised them to select among themselves a wise and prudent man, who, every morning and evening, should assemble them to offer to Almighty God their prayers and supplications. The meeting was held the very same evening, and the great chief promulgated a law that for the future the one who would be guilty of theft, or of other disorderly act, should receive a public castigation." This was the only occasion on which Father DeSmet met the Snake Indians. His subsequent trips to Oregon were, with one exception, by a different route.

8. Fervor of the Flatheads.

After spending a week at the Green River rendezvous, Father DeSmet and his Flathead guides, together with a dozen Canadians, started northward across the mountains which separate the headwaters of the Colorado from those of the Columbia. They crossed the historic Teton's Pass and came to the beautiful valley at the foot of the three Tetons, of which Father DeSmet has left a striking description. In this valley they found the camp of the Flatheads and their neighbors, the Pend d'Oreilles, numbering about 1,600 persons. DeSmet describes the affecting scenes of his meeting with these children of the wilderness:

"The poles were already up for my lodge, and at my approach, men, women and children came all to-

gether to meet me and shake hands and bid me welcome. The elders wept with joy, while the young men
expressed their satisfaction by leaps and shouts of happiness. These good savages led me to the lodge of the
old chief, called in his language, 'Big face.' He had
a truly patriarchal aspect and received me in the midst
of his whole council with the liveliest cordiality. Then
I had a long talk on religion with these honest folk. I
set a schedule of spiritual exercises for them, particularly for the morning and evening prayers in common and for hours of instruction.

"One of the chiefs at once brought me a bell to
give the signals, and on the first evening I gathered
all the people about my lodge; I said the evening
prayers, and finally they sang together, in a harmony
which surprised me very much, several songs of their
own composition on the praise of God. This zeal for
prayer and instruction (and I preached to them regularly four times a day) instead of declining, increased
up to the time of my departure."

DeSmet was wholly astonished at their fervor and
regularity at religious exercises. In speaking of this
subject on another occasion he exclaims: "Who would
not think that this could only be found in a well-or-
dered and religious community, and yet it is among the
Indians in the defiles and valleys of the Rocky Mountains." He was likewise astonished at the innocence
of their lives, and he has left pages of writing in which

he extols their virtues, and their docility. It would be difficult to find a parallel in the history of Christian missions for this rapid and permanent transformation of a savage tribe into a Christian community with morning and evening prayers in common.

9. At the Continental Divide.

The camp gradually moved up the Henry Fork of the Snake River to Lake Henry, one of the sources of the Columbia River. Here DeSmet climbed the mountain of the Continental Divide, whence he was able to see Red Rock Lake, the ultimate source of the Missouri. "The two lakes," he writes, "are scarce eight miles apart. I started for the summit of a high mountain for the better examination of the two fountains that gave birth to these two great rivers; I saw them falling in cascades from an immense height; hurling themselves with uproar from rock to rock; even at their source they formed two mighty torrents, scarcely more than a hundred paces apart. The Fathers of the Company who are in missionary service on the banks of the Mississippi, from Council Bluffs to the Gulf of Mexico, came to my mind." And his heart went out to the nations on the banks of the Columbia to whom the faith of Christ was yet to be preached. There he engraved on a soft stone, this inscription: "Sanctus Ignatius, Patronus Montium, Die Julii 23, 1840."

After two months among the Flatheads, DeSmet determined to return to St. Louis for assistance. He appointed a chief to take his place, to preside over the devotions and to baptize the children. He was accompanied by thirty warriors, among whom was the famous chief, Insula, whose futile trip to the rendezvous on the Green River in 1835 we have already mentioned. Father DeSmet reached St. Louis University on the last day of the year 1840. His first missionary journey to the nations of the Oregon country had been accomplished and, like another Paul, he returned rehearsing all the things that God had done with him, and how he had opened a door of faith to the nations.

10. The White Man's Book of Heaven.

Thirty-five years after the visit of the Indians to St. Louis (1831) the author of the Whitman myth, Rev. Mr. Spalding, evolved from his fertile but disordered imagination an account, which many have mistaken for serious history, of how the savages went to St. Louis in search of "the white man's Book of Heaven." Spalding begins the story (Sen. Ex. Doc. No. 37, 41st Cong., 3d Sess., on p. 8): "The Flatheads and Nez Perces had determined to send four of their number to the 'Rising Sun' for that Book from Heaven. They had got word of the Bible and a Saviour in some way from the Iroquois. . . . They fell into the hands of General Clark. He was a Romanist and took them to his church and to entertain them to the theatre. How utterly he failed to meet their wants is revealed in the sad words with which they departed." Then Barrows (*History of Oregon*) puts in quotation marks, as if its authenticity were undoubted, the following speech: " 'I came to you over a trail of many moons from the setting sun. You were the friend of my fathers who have all gone the long way. I came with one eye partly opened, for more light for my people, who sit in darkness. I go back with both eyes closed. How can I go back blind to my blind people? I made my way to you with strong arms, through many enemies and strange lands, that I might carry back much to them. I go back with both arms broken and empty. The two fathers who came with us — the braves of many winters and wars — we leave asleep here by your great water and wigwam. They were tired in many moons, and their moccasins wore out. My people sent me to get the white man's Book of Heaven. You took me where you allow your women to dance, as we do not ours, and the Book was not there. You took me where they worship the Great Spirit with candles, and the Book was not there. You showed me the images of good spirits and pictures of the good land beyond, but the Book was not among them to tell us the way. I am going back the long, sad trail to my people of the dark land. You make my feet heavy with burdens of gifts, and my moccasins will grow old in carrying them, but the Book is not among them. When I tell my poor, blind people, after one more snow, in the big council, that I did not bring the Book, no word will be spoken by our old men or by our young braves. One by one they will rise up and go out in silence. My people will die in darkness, and they will go on the long path to the other hunting grounds. No white man will go with them and no white man's Book to make the way plain. I have no more words.' "

Marshall, who has thoroughly exploded these claims of Spalding and Barrows, refers to the above as "the ridiculously improbable speech in which these half-naked savages, just emerging from the stone age of humanity are made to talk of the Bible and of the ceremonial of the Catholic Church 'where they worship the Great Spirit with candles,' etc., precisely as a very narrow-minded and intensely bigoted evangelical Protestant would do. It is as incredible that these Indians could have delivered any such speech as this, as it is that wild, uneducated Apaches or Hottentots or Esquimaux could intelligently discuss the relative merits of Buddhism and Christianity, or write an entertaining and instructive essay on the doctrine of evolution." Vol. 2, page 16.

"Not a trace of that impossible 'farewell speech' of the Flatheads to General Clark has ever been produced in print or in manuscript of an earlier date than February 16, 1866." Page 18.

Marshall has discovered that Clark was not only not a Catholic but was a prominent Mason. But facts were never a concern with the authors of the Whitman story.

The true account of the coming of the Indians to St. Louis was given by Bishop Rosati, December 31, 1831, to the editor of the *Annales de L'Association de la Propagation de la Foi* of Lyons, France. We have embodied the substance of it in the narrative of the preceding chapter.

NOTE. Capt. Bonneville found that the Nez Perces refused to hunt with him on Sunday, saying that, "it was a sacred day and the Great Spirit would be angry if they devoted it to hunting." On his arrival at Walla Walla, Pambrun informed Bonneville, says Irving, that "he (Pambrun) had been at some pains to introduce the Christian religion, and in the Roman Catholic form, among them, where it had evidently taken root . . . retaining the principal points of faith and its entire precepts of morality.

"Polygamy, which once prevailed among them to a great extent, was now rarely indulged. All the crimes denounced by the Christian faith met with severe punishment among them."

CHAPTER EIGHT

THE ROCKY MOUNTAIN MISSION

Courtesy of Hudson's Bay Company Officials. — Foundation of Bitter Root Mission. — Tribes of Northern Idaho Seek Aid. — Obstacles and Problems Incident to Work. — DeSmet at Fort Colville. — A Letter of Mrs. Whitman. — At Lake Pend d'Oreille

1. Courtesy of Hudson's Bay Company Officials.

On the feast of the Assumption, 1841, Father De-Smet had again penetrated the Oregon country as far as Fort Hall, on the Snake River. Fort Hall occupied a large place in early Oregon history. It was built by Nathaniel Wyeth, in 1834. Wyeth sold it to the Hudson's Bay Company two years later, and consequently at the time of DeSmet's visit it was under the direction of Dr. John McLoughlin, Chief Factor of the Hudson's Bay Company in Oregon. The local agent, Ermatinger, was prominent in the service of the Company, and his courtesy and generosity to DeSmet were only typical of the treatment accorded to the Catholic missionaries by the gentlemen of the Hudson's Bay Company at all of their forts during the McLoughlin régime. DeSmet spoke of Ermatinger in the following terms: "Although a Protestant by birth, this noble Englishman gave us a most friendly reception. Not only did he repeatedly invite us to his table, and sell us at first cost, or at one-third of its value, in a country so remote, whatever we required; but he also added as pure gifts many articles which he believed would be particularly acceptable — he assured us that he would second our ministry among the populous nation of the Snakes, with whom he had frequent intercourse."

2. Foundation of Bitter Root Mission.

When Father DeSmet met the Flatheads at Fort Hall on this occasion, he was better prepared to minister to their needs than on his former journey. He was accompanied by two priests and three brothers. The priests are well known in the early annals of Oregon. They were Fathers Nicholas Point and Gregory Mengarini. DeSmet had been successful, too, in securing financial aid for his missions. The Bishops and clergy of the dioceses of Philadelphia and New Orleans had responded very generously to his appeal. On reaching the Bitter Root Valley, the home of the Flathead tribe, DeSmet was thus enabled to lay the foundations of a permanent mission. He chose a location on the banks of the Bitter Root River, about twenty-eight miles above its mouth, between the site of old Fort Owen and the present town of Stevensville. St. Mary's Mission has had an eventful history. In 1850 it was closed temporarily, the improvements being leased to Major John Owen. Not until September, 1866, was the mission re-opened in charge of the venerated Father Ravalli. It is today a point of interest for the sightseer in the Bitter Root Valley.

3. Tribes of Northern Idaho Seek Aid.

While the work of establishing the mission was in progress, Father DeSmet received a delegation from the Coeur d'Alene nation. They had heard of his arrival among the Flatheads, and came to request his services. "Father," said one of them to him, "we are truly deserving of your pity. We wish to serve the Great Spirit, but we know not how. We want some one to teach us. For this reason we make application to you." Their wish was granted, and the little tribe received the Christian religion with the same zeal and devotion that the Flatheads had displayed. The Pend d'Oreilles, too, a numerous tribe who dwelt in what is now northern Idaho, welcomed the missionaries, as also did the Nez Perces. Father DeSmet had little hope of converting the Blackfeet. "They are the only Indians," he writes, "of whose salvation we would have reason to despair if the ways of God were the same as those of men, for they are murderers, thieves, traitors, and all that is wicked." Father Point subsequently established a successful mission among them.

4. Obstacles and Problems Incident to Work.

In establishing the Rocky Mountain missions, Father DeSmet and his companions had constant recourse to the experience of the Jesuit missionaries among the Indians of Paraguay. He expressly states that he made a *Vade Mecum* of the *Narrative of Muratori,* the historian of the Paraguay missions. The field west of the Rocky Mountains suggested to him many similarities with that among the native races of South America. The only obstacle to conversion in the one case as in the other, was the introduction of the vices of the whites. That alone stood in the way of the ultimate civilization of the natives. DeSmet refers to his missions as "reductions," a name borrowed from the South American system where it refers to the settlements which the missionaries induced their nomadic neophytes to adopt. He directed Father Point to draw up plans for the mission stations in conformity with the plans formerly adopted in the missions of Paraguay and described in detail by Muratori.

One of the problems that DeSmet had to meet at the outset, was that of Indian marriages. He acted on the principle that there were no valid marriages among the savages, and alleges the following reasons: "We had not found one, even among the best disposed, who after marriage has been contracted in their own fashion, did not believe himself justified in sending away his first wife whenever he thought fit and taking another. Many even have several wives at the same time. We are then agreed on this principle, that among them, even to the present time, there has been no marriage, because they have never known well in what its essence and obligation consisted." Consequently, immediately after the ceremony of baptism, the marriage ceremony was performed, after the necessary instruction had been given. This procedure gave rise to various interesting situations. "Many who had two wives have retained her whose children were the most numerous, and with all possible respect dismissed the other." Father DeSmet tells of one savage who followed his advice and dismissed his youngest wife, giving her what he would have wished another to give to his sister, if in the same situation, and was reunited to his first wife whom he had forsaken.

5. DeSmet at Fort Colville.

During the closing months of 1841, DeSmet undertook a journey from the Bitter Root Valley to Fort Colville on the Columbia. On All Saints' Day he met two encampments of the Kalispel nation, who were to be a great consolation to the missionary. The chief of the first camp was the famous Chalax. Although they had never seen a priest before, they knew all the prayers DeSmet had taught the Flatheads. This is a striking illustration of the religious sentiment among the Oregon Indians of the Interior. Their knowledge of these prayers is thus explained by DeSmet: "They had deputed an intelligent young man, who was gifted with a good memory, to meet me. Having learned the prayers and canticles and such points as were most essential for salvation, he repeated to the village all that he had heard and seen. It was, as you can easily imagine, a great consolation for me to see the sign of the cross and hear prayers addressed to the great God and His praises sung in a desert of about three hundred miles extent, where a Catholic priest had never been before."

6. A Letter of Mrs. Whitman.

The Kalispels had been visited during the summer by ministers who had attempted to disaffect the minds of the savages toward the Catholic missionaries. The Indians' natural and instinctive reverence for the blackrobe, however, soon overcame the prejudice instilled by the hostile ministers. Interesting light is thrown on the missionary situation at this time by a private letter of the wife of the leader of the American Board Mission. Mrs. Whitman, writing in 1842, and faithfully reflecting the sentiments of her husband, considered that the interests of the Oregon country hung in the balance with the "prosperity of the cause of Christ on the one hand and the extension of the powers and dominions of Romanism on the other." She continues: "Romanism stalks abroad on our right hand and on our left, and with daring effrontery, boasts that she is to prevail and possess the land. I ask, must it be so? The zeal and energy of her priests are without a parallel, and many, both white men and Indians, wander after the beasts. Two are in the country below us and two are above in the mountains." The priests below at Vancouver were Fathers Blanchet and Demers; those above were DeSmet and Point. Narcissa Whitman bears striking testimony to their zeal and energy. With this letter before us we shall not be surprised to learn that when Dr. Whitman and his wife were massacred by the Indians in 1847, his co-workers were in a temper to lay the blame for the outrage at the door of the Catholic missionaries.

7. At Lake Pend d'Oreille.

Father DeSmet's journey to Fort Colville led him past the beautiful Lake Pend d'Oreille and the magnificent forest at its head. He was an ardent lover of nature and the record he has left of his impressions on beholding this splendid scene is typical of his many descriptions of nature. "At the head of Lake Pend d'Oreille," he writes, "we traversed a forest which is certainly a wonder of its kind; there is probably nothing similar to it in America. The birch, elm and beech, generally small elsewhere, like the toad of La Fontaine that aimed at being as large as the ox, swell out here to twice their size. They would fain rival the cedar, the Goliath of the forest, who, however, looking down with contempt upon his pitiful companions,

> 'Eleve aux cieux
> Son front audacieux.'

The birch and the beech at its side, resemble large candelabra around a massive column. Cedars of four and five fathoms in circumference are here very common. The delicate branches of these noble trees entwine themselves above the beech and elm; their fine, dense and evergreen foliage forming an arch through which the sun's rays never penetrate; and this lofty arch, supported by thousands of columns, brought to the mind's eye the idea of an immense temple reared by the hand of nature to the glory of its author."

He reached Fort Colville about the middle of November and received a very hearty welcome from the commandant, Archibald Macdonald. Fort Colville was one of the Hudson's Bay Company's stations. Macdonald had been in the employ of the company for many years, having founded Fort Nesqually, until 1907 the nominal seat of the present Catholic Diocese of Seattle. The reception given to DeSmet at Fort Hall was repeated at Fort Colville, and our missionary voices the general sentiment of his co-workers when he takes occasion of Macdonald's hospitality to write: "Whenever one finds the gentlemen of the Hudson's Bay Company, one is sure of a good reception. They do not stop with demonstrations of politeness and affability; they anticipate your wishes in order to be of service to you." The record is the same at Forts Vancouver and Hall, Colville and Nesqually, Okanogan and Walla Walla, and the rest. No doubt the influence of Dr. McLoughlin was the determining factor in the attitude of the Company.

NOTE. To the effectiveness of the work of the Catholic missionaries, Snowden in his *History of Washington* bears the following testimony (Vol. II, p. 167):

"The Catholic missionaries acquired and retained over the native population west of the Rocky Mountains a far more perfect control than the Protestant missionaries were ever able to secure. Dissensions such as disturbed the harmony of the other missions were among them impossible. Secular matters never diverted the priests from their work. As soon as they were sufficiently numerous an ecclesiastical superior was appointed to have charge and direct their work, and his authority was supreme....

"The zealous priests, always rendering implicit obedience to their ecclesiastical head, troubled themselves about nothing that did not concern the work they were sent to do. They everywhere met a welcome from the Indians such as was rarely given to the Protestants. The 'Black-gowns,' as the Indians called them, were always popular."

REINFORCEMENTS FROM EUROPE

I. At the Coeur d'Alene Camp.

Returning to his mission in the Bitter Root Valley,
in December, 1841, with the provisions and implements secured at Fort Colville, Father DeSmet spent
the winter among his Flathead neophytes. In April,
of the following year, he set out on his first visit to
Fort Vancouver and the Willamette Valley, a journey
of a thousand miles. In the course of his travel on this
occasion he evangelized whole villages of Kootenais,
Kalispels, Coeur d'Alenes, Spokanes and Okanogans,
establishing in almost every case the practice of morning and evening prayers in each village. He found the
Coeur d'Alene camp at the outlet of the great lake
which bears their name. The entire camp turned out
to welcome him. An extract from one of his letters
will show how eagerly they listened to his words: "I
spoke to them for two hours on salvation and the end of

man's creation, and not one person stirred from his place during the whole time of instruction. As it was almost sunset, I recited the prayers I had translated into their language a few days before. At their own request I then continued instructing the chiefs and their people until the night was far advanced. About every half hour I paused, and then the pipes would pass round to refresh the listeners and give time for reflection." Never did DeSmet experience more satisfaction among the Indians as on this occasion, and nowhere were his efforts crowned with greater and more permanent success. The Coeur d'Alenes have still the reputation of being the best and most industrious Indians in the Rocky Mountains.

2. Meeting of Fathers Blanchet and DeSmet.

The journey from Fort Colville to Fort Vancouver was marred by an unfortunate accident. At one of the rapids of the Columbia, the barge containing DeSmet's effects capsized, and all the crew, save three, were drowned. Providentially, Father DeSmet had gone ashore, intending to walk along the bank while the bargemen directed the boat through the rapids. After brief visits at Forts Okanogan and Walla Walla, he hastened on to Vancouver, where he received a most affecting welcome from the pioneer Catholic missionaries of the Oregon country, Blanchet and Demers. The latter has related how Blanchet and DeSmet ran to meet each other, both prostrating themselves, each begging the other's blessing. It was a meeting fraught with important consequences for the Catholic Church in Oregon.[1]

3. Missionary Conference at Vancouver.

In his *Historical Sketches,* Archbishop Blanchet gives us a few details in addition to those mentioned in DeSmet's *Letters,* from which it appears that Father

---

1. Father Blanchet had been hardly a year in the Oregon Country when he began to realize the importance of having a bishop located on the lower Columbia in charge of the missions. His first thought, as expressed in a letter to the Coadjutor Bishop of Quebec under date of March 19, 1840, was that Bishop Provencher of Red River should be transferred to Vancouver. When Father DeSmet came to St. Paul in 1842, the question of the establishment of a diocese was the principal topic discussed by the two missionaries, and their conference led to taking immediate steps towards that end. Father DeSmet went back to St. Louis to bring the matter to the attention of the ecclesiastical authorities; while Father Blanchet wrote both to Bishop Rosati (June 20, 1842) and to Bishop Signay of Quebec (June 24, 1842) urging immediate collaboration between them with a view to appointing a bishop for the Oregon Country. He strongly represented to Bishop Signay his own unfitness for the office, and suggested the appointment of DeSmet.

As a result while the American and the Canadian bishops joined in petitioning the Holy See for the establishment of an ecclesiastical government on the lower Columbia, Bishop Signay recommended that a diocese be constituted with Blanchet as bishop, whereas Bishop Kenrick, Auxiliary Bishop of St. Louis, acting on the recommendation of the bishops of the Provincial Council of Baltimore (1843) proposed the erection of a vicariate with Father DeSmet as vicar apostolic. (For the appointment of Blanchet see Chapter X, Section 8.) The correspondence referred to above is in the archives of the Archdiocese of Quebec; copies are in the possession of Mr. John P. O'Hara through the courtesy of Msgr. Peter Guilday. See also letters of the Bishops of St. Louis and Quebec reprinted in Garraghan, *The Jesuits of the Middle United States,* Volume II ("The Oregon Mission").

Demers met the Jesuit missionary at Fort Vancouver and conducted him to the residence of the Vicar General at St. Paul. DeSmet returned to Vancouver with Father Demers, followed a few days later by Father Blanchet, "to deliberate on the interests of the great mission of the Pacific Coast." At the conference it was decided that Father Demers should proceed to open a mission in New Caledonia (now British Columbia), leaving the Vicar General at St. Paul, while DeSmet should start for St. Louis and Belgium in quest of more workers and material assistance for the missions of Oregon. Dr. McLoughlin, though not yet a Catholic, strongly encouraged Father DeSmet to make every effort to increase the number of Catholic missionaries. On June 30, 1842, DeSmet bade farewell to his new friends at Fort Vancouver, and set out for the East to secure recruits and supplies for the Oregon missions.

4. DeSmet Returns With Reinforcements.

Twenty-five months elapsed before Father DeSmet returned again to Fort Vancouver. After visiting many of the chief cities of Europe, he set sail from Antwerp on the brig, Infatigable, early in January, 1844, accompanied by four Fathers and a lay brother of the Society, and six Sisters of Notre Dame de Namur. The Infatigable rounded Cape Horn on March 20, 1844, and came in sight of the Oregon coast on July 28. After a terrifying experience they crossed the Columbia bar in safety on July 31, the feast of St. Ignatius. Father DeSmet frequently refers to the "divine pilotage" which brought them unharmed through the shallow passage and the treacherous breakers. From Astoria, DeSmet set out for Vancouver in a canoe, leaving his companions to follow when a favorable wind would permit. He was received with open arms by Dr. McLoughlin and by Father Demers, who was planning to leave shortly for Canada to secure Sisters to open a school. From Father Demers he received the good news that the missionaries in the Rocky Mountains had received a strong reinforcement from St. Louis during his absence. The Vicar General, Father Blanchet, was at St. Paul when informed of DeSmet's arrival. He immediately set out for Vancouver, bringing a number of his parishioners with him and traveling all night by canoe.

5. Celebrates the Feast of the Assumption.

On the eve of the feast of the Assumption, the newly-arrived recruits for the mission left Fort Vancouver for St. Paul. "Our little squadron," says Father DeSmet, "consisted of four canoes manned by the parishioners of Father Blanchet, and our own sloop. We sailed up the river and soon entered the Willamette. As night approached, we moored our vessels and encamped upon the shore. (This must have been within the limits of the present city of Portland.) The morning's dawn found us on foot. It was the festival of the glorious Assumption of the Mother of God. Aided by the nuns, I erected a small altar. Father Blanchet offered the Holy Sacrifice, at which all communicated. Finally, the 17th, about 11 o'clock, we came in sight of our dear mission of Willamette. A cart was procured to conduct the nuns to their dwelling, which is about five miles from the river. In two hours we were all assembled in the chapel of Willamette, to adore and thank our Divine Saviour by the solemn chanting of the *Te Deum*."

6. St. Francis Xavier Mission Founded.

On arriving at St. Paul, DeSmet's first care was to seek a convenient location for what was intended to be the base of missionary activities in Oregon. The Methodists offered to sell him their academy, which they had decided to close. Ten years had passed since Jason and Daniel Lee founded the Methodist mission in the Willamette Valley; a large sum of money had been expended in the enterprise, but as an Indian mission it was confessedly a failure. Hence it was decided to suppress it and sell all the property in 1844. Father DeSmet, however, secured a more advantageous location, where he laid the foundations of the St. Francis Xavier Mission on the Willamette.

CHAPTER TEN

DEVELOPMENTS — ECCLESIASTICAL AND POLITICAL

Father Demers Visits Fort St. James. — Douglas Founds Victoria. — Chapel Planned for Oregon City. — Political Situation in 1840. — Meeting to Form Provisional Government. — McLoughlin's Contribution to Settlement of Oregon Question. — Blanchet's Attitude Towards American Government. — Father Blanchet Consecrated Bishop. — Summary of Six Years' Apostolic Work

I. Father Demers Visits Fort St. James.

The lives of the missionaries were eventful enough during these years. Father Demers carried the standard of the faith far north to Fort Langley on the Fraser River. Missions were opened for the Indians at the Clackamas, Willamette Falls (Oregon City), and Cascade settlements by the Vicar General. The work was growing apace. The score of establishments from Fort Colville on the Columbia to St. Paul on the Willamette and Fort Langley on the Fraser were taxing the strength of the two zealous laborers. A new field of missionary activity was proposed among the tribes of New Caledonia (British Columbia), and Father Demers was dispatched to lay the foundations. Demers pushed north, after leaving the boats at Fort Walla Walla, past Fort

Alexander on the Fraser River to Fort St. James on
Stuart Lake, several hundred miles north of Fort Vancouver. Chief Factor Peter Skene Ogden, who, a few
years later, succeeded McLoughlin at Vancouver and
was so prominent in the rescue of the survivors of the
Whitman massacre, was in charge of Fort St. James.
Mrs. Ogden[1] was a Catholic, and through her kindness
Father Demers found a more hospitable welcome than
he could have anticipated. He celebrated High Mass
at Fort St. James on September 16, 1842, in a region
hitherto outside the limits of Christianity. Before the
end of the year he was back to Fort Alexander, where
he had a chapel erected by the Indians. In the spring
of 1843 he returned to civilization in company with
Chief Factor Ogden, riding on horseback from Fort
Alexander through three or four feet of snow.

2. Douglas Founds Victoria.

In the meantime recruits had come to rejoice the
heart and aid the labors of the Vicar General. On September 17, 1842, Fathers Langlois and Bolduc arrived

---

1. The influence of the Hudson's Bay Company's officials in
their dealings with the Indians was due in no small measure to their
Indian wives. This was true in the case of Dr. McLoughlin, and
even to a more notable degree in regard to Ogden, who had married
an Indian princess. By blood and marriage Princess Julia was related to every important chief of the Northwest, making it safe for
her husband to travel where no one else would dare to go. Ogden,
married according to Indian custom, refused even when dying to
have a civil marriage ceremony, declaring it would be a reflection
on his past conduct. As a result Mrs. Ogden came into possession
of his property only after extended litigation.

at St. Paul from Canada via Boston and Cape Horn. On the following day (Sunday) High Mass was celebrated with deacon and subdeacon for the first time in Oregon Country. The new missionaries were not long in finding employment. Chief Factor Douglas set out in March, 1843, to found Victoria on the south end of Vancouver Island. He was accompanied by Father Bolduc. The party went to Fort Nesqually, where they took the steamer, Beaver, for their destination. On Sunday, March 19, Father Bolduc celebrated Mass in the presence of more than one thousand Indians at the newly-founded Victoria, and baptized over one hundred of their children.

3. Chapel Planned for Oregon City.

Meanwhile the Vicar General had bought a lot at Willamette Falls (Oregon City), where he proposed that Father Langlois should build a chapel for the Indians. Dr. McLoughlin had spent the month of December, 1842, in platting his new townsite of Oregon City at Willamette Falls. Settlers began to come in rapidly, and the Indian congregation consequently melted away with even greater rapidity, much to the disappointment of Father Langlois. Three years later Oregon City was to witness the erection of the first Cathedral in the Pacific Northwest.

4. Political Situation in 1840.

While Father Blanchet was zealously directing the spiritual affairs of the vast territory committed to his care, political changes were taking place which brought him temporarily into public view. To understand his attitude towards the provisional government, we must take a hasty survey of the political situation of the time. The Oregon country was in a state of "joint occupancy"; that is, the dividing line between British and American possessions had not yet been determined, and under a convention of 1818, again renewed in 1827, the country was to be "free and open to the vessels, citizens and subjects of the two powers." They were not, however, equally protected. The powerful Hudson's Bay Company exercised police protection over the British subjects and the English Parliament had extended the Colonial jurisdiction and civil laws of Canada over all British subjects on the coast. As for the American settlers, a writer has appropriately applied to them the words: "In those days there was no king in Israel and everyone did whatsoever was right in his own eyes." In 1840 a number of the American emigrants addressed a petition to Congress asking that body to extend the protection of American civil institution over Oregon.

5. Meeting to Form Provisional Government.

There was no prospect of favorable action by Congress when an event occurred which brought the necessity of a civil government again before the minds of the American settlers. On February 15, 1841, Ewing Young, the pioneer stockman of the Willamette Valley, died intestate. A meeting was called to settle the disposition of the estate. At this meeting it was recommended that a committee be appointed to draft a constitution and a code of laws for the government of the settlement south of the Columbia River, and a resolution was passed that settlers north of the Columbia not connected with the Hudson's Bay Company might be admitted to the protection of the laws of the proposed government. Another meeting was called for the next day to elect officers and to select the committee. The committee appointed on the following day was headed by Father Blanchet as chairman, contrary to his own wishes. The selection of Father Blanchet for this position was doubtless due to a desire to gain the support of the Canadian settlers for the proposed government, there being in the entire settlement at this time about one hundred and forty Americans and sixty Canadians. The Canadians were, as we have said, protected by the Canadian government and were in a special manner indebted to the Hudson's Bay Company. They were, for the most part, old employes of the Company and had received material assistance from Dr. McLoughlin since their retirement from service. The committee was to report at a meeting on June 1 following, but when

the appointed time arrived Father Blanchet announced
that he had not called the committee together and
asked to be excused from serving as chairman, not
having time to devote to the work. For this act Father
Blanchet has been severely handled by partisan historians of Oregon. W. H. Gray, in his so-called *History
of Oregon,* is especially abusive. Chief Justice Burnett,
in his manuscript, *Memoirs of an Old Pioneer* (in the
Bancroft Library), defends Blanchet's action on the
ground that he did not feel equal to the work which
the committee had been set to do. It seems more prob-
able, however, that Father Blanchet did not approve
of the plan, both because of its small chance of success
and because of the attitude of its promoters towards the
Hudson's Bay Company. The impracticable character
of the proposed government may be learned from the
fact that the committee accomplished no more under
Blanchet's successor than it had before. The project
was opposed by Lieutenant Wilkes, who was at Vancouver at this time in charge of the American exploring expedition on the Pacific.

6. McLoughlin's Contribution to Settlement of Oregon Question.

Moreover, the animus of the promoters of the movement doomed it to failure. Opposition to the Hudson's
Bay Company was the ruling passion with the men who
were projecting the new government. This was ob-

vious to Father Blanchet, and his relations with Dr. McLoughlin made it impossible for him to concur in the movement. The events in Oregon from 1840 to 1844 which laid the foundation of American ascendency in this region were not political meetings or petitions to Congress reciting (falsely) the tyrannous exactions of the Hudson's Bay Company. American supremacy was established during this period by the annual influx of immigrants whose settlement in Oregon was made possible by the grand humanity of old Dr. McLoughlin, who extended over them his protecting hand, saving them from the savages and from famine, caring for their sick, furnshing them supplies of food and clothing and shelter for the winter and providing them with seed grain for the spring; and all this, let it be remembered, at his own loss, contrary to the express orders of his Company and in spite of the calumnies which the Americans already in the country were spreading concerning him.

7. Blanchet's Attitude Towards American Government.

On the occasion of the third annual reunion of the Oregon Pioneer Association in 1876, the annual address was delivered by the Hon. Matthew P. Deady. In the course of his address, Judge Deady, after very correctly observing that the Catholic missionaries were indifferent as to the ultimate possession of the country, because they were not settlers but ministers of the Gospel, continued as follows: "They (Blanchet and Demers) were, however, subjects of Great Britain, and their influence and teaching among the people was naturally in favor of the authority and interest of the Hudson's Bay Company. They discouraged the early attempts at the formation of a settlers' government in the country." Archbishop Blanchet, in his *Historical Sketches* (1878), characterizes this statement as "a great mistake," and adds (page 122), "All this is entirely inaccurate; their being British subjects had nothing to do with their teaching, nor would it naturally lead them 'to teach their people in favor of the authority and interest of a fur-company.' A higher sense of feeling than this was their rule; they had a conscience and a faith. Nor did they ever discourage the early attempts of a settlers' government, either within or without their churches. When during the meeting in June, 1841, Vicar General Blanchet gave his opinion that it was too soon (and), that as Commodore Wilkes was expected here, the committee should wait for his opinion — that step was by no means an act of opposition, but on the contrary an act of prudence which the Commodore approved of at St. Paul on June 7th, on the ground that the country was too young. And also on a later occasion when he begged that his name be erased from those of the committee, that was done in no sense out of opposition but for want of time. In a word, let all comprehend that the two Catholic missionaries understood too well the delicacy of their position in this new and unsettled country to commit such imprudent blunders." It is clear, however, from an unpublished letter of Father Blanchet to Governor Simpson under date of November 15, 1841, that he was opposed to the proposal for a local government at the time for the reasons we have already assigned.

8. Father Blanchet Consecrated Bishop.

While these political developments were taking place, a change in ecclesiastical administration was likewise being effected. The Bishops of Quebec and Baltimore, acting in concert (it will be recalled that the Oregon country was in a state of joint occupancy, and ecclesiastical as well as civil limits were ill-defined), recommended to the Holy See to erect the joint mission into a vicariate apostolic. The suggestion was accepted, and by a brief of December 1, 1843, the new vicariate was created with Father Blanchet as its Vicar Apostolic with the title of Philadelphia *in partibus* (subsequently changed to that of Drasa to avoid confusion). The news of this action did not reach Oregon until November 4 of the following year. The Bishop-elect decided to go to Canada for the purpose of receiving episcopal consecration. Appointing Father Demers administrator, Father Blanchet crossed the Columbia bar December 5, 1844, on a ship bearing the name of the river. The voyage to Montreal was by a circuitous route.

The ship visited Honolulu, doubled Cape Horn and arrived at Deal, England. Father Blanchet then went to Liverpool, where he embarked for Boston. He reached Montreal towards the end of June, after a tedious journey of more than six months.[1] Here on July 25, 1845, he received his consecration at the hands of the Right Rev. Ignatius Bourget, Bishop of Montreal.

9. Summary of Six Years' Apostolic Work.

A little more than six years had elapsed since Father Blanchet had established the Oregon Mission. Casting a retrospective glance over those years of missionary activity, he writes in his *Historical Sketches:* "At the end of 1844, after six years of efforts disproportioned to the needs of the country, the vast mission of Oregon, on the eve of its being erected into a vicariate apostolic, had gained nearly all of the Indian tribes of the (Puget) Sound, Caledonia (British Columbia) and

---

1. Snowden tells the following interesting story: "Early in November Father Blanchet received notice that Oregon had been made a vicariate apostolic, of which he was to be the ecclesiastical head, with the title of Bishop of Philadelphia.... Upon reflection, and consideration of the difficulties of the journey, and the time he would need to be absent, he concluded to go to Mexico (to be consecrated). But on arriving there, he found that while the notice of his appointment was regular, and its genuineness undoubted, the canonical law required his own identification as the person for whom the appointment had been made. As identification was impossible where nobody could be found who had ever seen him before, he went to France, but found the same difficulty there. He accordingly crossed the Atlantic again to Canada, where, at Montreal, the city from which he had been sent out to the West seven years earlier as a missionary priest, the pioneer head of the Catholic Church in Oregon was duly consecrated." (*History of Washington,* Vol. II, p. 166.)

several tribes of the Rocky Mountains and of Lower Oregon. It had brought six thousand pagans to the faith. Nine missions had been founded; five in lower Oregon and four at the Rocky Mountains. Eleven churches and chapels had been erected, five in lower Oregon, two in Caledonia, and four at the Rocky Mountains. One thousand Canadians, women and children, had been saved from the imminent perils of losing their faith. . . . The Catholic Mission possessed two educational establishments, one for boys and the other for girls; the number of its missionaries had been raised to fifteen, without speaking of the treasure of the mission had in the persons of the good Religieuses of Notre Dame de Namur" (p. 123). We have in this brief record of the labors of our missionary priest an earnest of the apostolic work that was yet to be wrought by his consecrated hands.

CHAPTER ELEVEN

CLOSE OF DESMET'S OREGON MISSION

I. Prosperity of Flathead Mission.

In June, 1846, DeSmet was back again at Fort Colville, and was there joined by Father Nobili, who had just returned from a missionary journey to Fort St. James, the capital of New Caledonia, situated on Stuart Lake. The end of June saw him at St. Francis Xavier mission on the Willamette. A few weeks later he was making his way up the Columbia in an Indian canoe with two blankets unfurled by way of sails. At Walla Walla he experienced the hospitality of Mr. McBean, the superintendent of the Fort. Taking farewell of Mr. McBean, Father DeSmet visited the Nez Perces, Kalispels and Coeur d'Alenes, among whom were stationed Fathers Hoeken, Joset and Point. On the Feast of the Assumption, he was again among the Flatheads in the Bitter Root Valley. St. Mary's mission had prospered, both materially and spiritually. He found the little log church, which had been erected five years before, about to be replaced by a large and handsome structure. Another agreeable surprise awaited him. The mechanical skill of Father Ravalli had erected a flour mill and a saw mill. "The flour mill," writes Father DeSmet, "grinds ten or twelve bushels a day, and the saw mill furnishes an abundant supply of planks, posts, etc., for the public and private building of the nation settled here."

2. DeSmet's Influence Among the Indians.

On August 16, 1846, Father DeSmet left St. Mary's mission in the Bitter Root and reached the University of St. Louis December 10. His missionary work in Oregon was at an end. His biographers, summing up this period of his career, write as follows: "The results of his labors from a missionary point of view, were highly successful. The whole Columbia Valley had been dotted with infant establishments, some of which had taken on the promise of permanent growth. He had, indeed, laid the foundation well for a spiritual empire throughout that region, and but for the approach of emigration, his plans would have brought forth the full fruition that he expected. But most important of all, from a public point of view, was the fact that he had become a great power among the Indian tribes. All now knew him, many personally, the rest by reputation. He was the one white man in whom they had implicit faith. The government was beginning to look to him for assistance. The Mormon, the forty-niner, the Oregon emigrant, came to him for information and advice. His writings were already known on two continents and his name was a familiar one, at least in the religious world."

3. The Yakima Outbreak.

Father DeSmet paid two subsequent visits to the scenes of his missionary labors in Oregon. The first of these visits was occasioned by the Indian outbreak in 1855, known as the Yakima War. The savages, viewing with alarm the encroachments of the whites upon their lands, formed a league to repel the invaders. Even the peaceful Flatheads and Coeur d'Alenes joined the coalition. The United States government sent General Harney, who had won distinction in several Indian wars, to take charge of the situation. At the personal request of General Harney, Father DeSmet was selected to accompany the expedition in the capacity of chaplain. Their party reached Vancouver late in October, 1858. The news of the cessation of hostilities and the submission of the Indians had already reached the fort. But the Indians, though subdued, were still unfriendly, and there was constant danger of a fresh outbreak. The work of pacification was still to be effected. Upon this mission DeSmet left Vancouver, under orders of the commanding general, to visit the mountain tribes some 800 miles distant.

4. DeSmet as a Peace Maker.

He visited the Catholic soldiers at Fort Walla Walla, and there met Father Congiato, superior of the mission, from whom he received favorable information concerning the dispositions of the tribes in the mountains. By the middle of April, 1859, Father DeSmet had revisited practically all the tribes among whom he had labored as a missionary. On April 16, he left the mission of St. Ignatius, among the Pend d'Oreilles, to return to Fort Vancouver. He was accompanied, at his own request, by the chiefs of the different mountain tribes, with the view of renewing the treaty of peace with the General and with the Superintendent of Indian affairs. The successful issue of Father DeSmet's mission is seen from a letter of General Harney, dated Fort Vancouver, June 1, 1859. He writes: "I have the honor to report, for the information of the General-in-Chief, the arrival at this place of a deputation of Indian chiefs, on a visit suggested by myself through the kind offices of the Reverend Father DeSmet, who has been with these tribes the past winter. These chiefs have all declared to me the friendly desires which now animate them towards our people. Two of these chiefs — one of the upper Pend d'Oreilles, and the other of the Flatheads — report that the proudest boast of their respective tribes is the fact that no white man's blood has ever been shed by any one of either nation. This statement is substantiated by Father DeSmet. It gives me pleasure to commend to the General-in-Chief the able and efficient services the Reverend Father DeSmet has rendered." Having fulfilled his mission, DeSmet secured his release from the post of chaplain and returned to St. Louis, visiting a score of Indian tribes on the way. It is typical of him that he should have planned, despite his three score years, to cover the entire distance from Vancouver to St. Louis on horseback, a project which he was regretfully compelled to abandon because of the unfitness of his horses for so long a journey.

5. Bids Farewell to Oregon Country.

Once more, in 1863, DeSmet traversed the Oregon Country, renewing his acquaintances with the various missions and enjoying the hospitality of the three pioneer bishops of the province, at Portland, Vancouver, Washington and Victoria, B. C. DeSmet's missionary labors in Oregon had come to a close before the arrival of Bishop A. M. A. Blanchet in the Pacific Northwest. Both Archbishop Blanchet and Bishop Demers were co-apostles with him in this new corner of the Lord's vineyard, and with him had borne the burden of the pioneer work. Now, however, the pioneer days were over, and DeSmet, as he set sail from Portland on October 13, 1863, could bear witness to the altered aspect of the country. But with all the signs of progress about him, there was one undeniable feature of the situation which brought sadness to his heart. The Indian tribes for whom he had labored with such apostolic zeal, the children of the forest, whose wonderful disposition for Christian faith and Christian virtue had been his consolation and his glory, were doomed. The seed of the Gospel, which he had sown, had taken root and sprung up and was blossoming forth with the promise of an abundant harvest when the blight came. The white man was in the land. The Indian envied his strength and imitated his vices and fell before both. "May heaven preserve them from the dangerous contact with the whites!" was DeSmet's last prayer for his neophytes as he bade farewell to the Oregon Country.

6. DeSmet's Views on the Oregon Question.

An interesting incident early in August, 1845, brings Father DeSmet's views of public affairs to our attention. The "Oregon Question" was then the all-absorbing theme. While DeSmet was ascending the Clark River, he had an unexpected interview on this subject. As he was approaching the forest on the shore of Lake Pend d'Oreille, several horsemen issued from its depths, and the foremost among them saluted him by name. On nearer approach Father DeSmet recognized Peter Skene Ogden, one of the leading representatives of the Hudson's Bay Company. Ogden was accompanied by two English officers, Warre and Vavasour. DeSmet was alarmed by the information he obtained from the travelers regarding the Oregon question. He writes: "They were invested with orders from their government to take possession of Cape Disappointment, to hoist the English standard, and to erect a fortress for the purpose of securing the entrance of the river in case of war. In the 'Oregon Question,' John Bull, without much talk attains his end and secures the most important part of the country; whereas Uncle Sam loses himself in words, inveighs and storms! Many years have passed in debates and useless contention without one single practical effort to secure his real or pretended rights."

Some writers have gathered from those expressions that Father DeSmet was hostile to the claims of our country, and would have preferred to see the Oregon Country fall under British sovereignty. This view was given wide circulation by the Protestant missionaries. For example, Dr. Whitman writes from Wailatpu, under date of November 5, 1846: "The Jesuit Papists would have been in quiet possession of this, the only spot in the Western horizon of America, not before their own. It would have been but a small work for them and the friends of the English interests, which they had also fully avowed, to have routed us, and then the country might have slept in their hands forever." The truth is, of course, quite the contrary to these representations. What Father DeSmet feared was that Oregon might be lost to the United States, at least temporarily, by indecision on the part of our government.

In a letter to Senator Benton, written in 1849, De-
Smet recounts a conversation which he had with several
British officers on the brig, Modeste, before Fort Vancouver, in 1846, in which his attitude towards the Oregon question is made clear. The party was discussing
the possibility of the English taking possession, not
merely of Oregon, but of California as well. Father
DeSmet ventured the opinion that such a conquest was
a dream not easily realized, and went on to remark that
should the English take possession of Oregon for the
moment, it would be an easy matter for the Americans to cross the mountains and wrest the entire country from them almost without a blow. On learning
these sentiments, the captain asked DeSmet somewhat
warmly, "Are you a Yankee?" "Not a born one, Captain," was his reply, "but I have the good luck of being
a naturalized American for these many years past; and
in these matters all my good wishes are for the side of
my adopted country."

CHAPTER TWELVE

THE ORIGINAL OREGON LAND FRAUD

McLoughlin's Land Claim Disputed. — The Oregon
Donation Land Act.—Thurston's Calumnies.—Friends
and Enemies Pass Resolutions. — Last Years of Mc-
Loughlin. — Tribute to the Memory of McLoughlin

1. McLoughlin's Land Claim Disputed.

Before McLoughlin retired to Oregon City in 1846,
his land claim had been disputed by members of the
Methodist Mission. Later years have brought into prom-
inence the Oregon land frauds. The events which we
shall now narrate may well be called the "original
Oregon land fraud."

In 1829, several years before the arrival of any of
the mission party, McLoughlin had taken possession
for himself as a personal claim, of the present site of
Oregon City with the water power at the falls of the
Willamette River and also of an island situated near
the crest of the falls, later known as Governor's Island,
but now called Abernethy Island. The position of the
island made it extremely valuable for the use of water
power. It is now the site of a station of the Portland
General Electric Company. In 1829, Dr. McLoughlin
began the erection of a saw mill at the falls. Three

years later he had a mill race blasted out of the rocks at the head of the island. In 1840 Rev. Jason Lee, superintendent of the Methodist Mission, applied to him for the loan of some timbers with which to erect the mission building. McLoughlin gave him the timbers and a piece of land on which to build. Within a short time after the arrival of the ship Lausanne, in 1840, with the "great reinforcement" for the Methodist Mission, there appeared a disposition on the part of Rev. Alvin Waller, who was given charge of the local mission near Oregon City, to defraud McLoughlin of his land claim. The following year another representative of the mission, named Hathaway, began to build on the island. McLoughlin protested and Hathaway ceased building. In 1842 McLoughlin became a Catholic. He spent the month of December of that year on his claim laying it out into blocks and lots and gave it the name "Oregon City." Five days after McLoughlin's conversion, Hathaway deeded the island to the Oregon Milling Company, most of the members of which belonged to the Methodist Mission. By this deed Hathaway conveyed to that company all his "rights" (sic) to the island, and further undertook to defend the title against "all persons (the Lord excepted)." Of course, Hathaway had absolutely no "right" to the island. He had "jumped" McLoughlin's claim. The island was subsequently "conveyed" to Governor Abernethy; whence the name Abernethy Island. In 1849 Abernethy in turn conveyed his title to the island to W. P. Bryant, the first territorial Chief Justice of Oregon. Judge Bryant's district included Oregon City. One can readily see what chance of legal redress now remained. While Hathaway was religiously conveying rights and titles to an island he never owned, the Rev. Alvin Waller retained legal counsel and laid claim to all of the rest of McLoughlin's land. In order to avoid trouble McLoughlin bought up Waller's ridiculous pretensions. For the consideration of five hundred dollars Waller surrendered to McLoughlin "all claims, rights and pretensions whatsoever" to the tract of land in dispute. This was in 1844. Apparently the trouble was definitely settled; in reality it had just begun.

2. The Oregon Donation Land Act.

The conspiracy against McLoughlin assumed definite form in 1849, when Samuel Thurston was elected Territorial Delegate to Congress from Oregon through the efforts of the Mission Party. The legislation in which Oregon was chiefly interested at that time was the passage of a land bill by which settlers could obtain a legal title to their land. With Thurston manipulating this piece of legislation, we come to the event we have called the original Oregon land fraud. The Oregon Donation Land Bill, the passage of which was urged by Thurston, was so framed as to secure to the early settlers a title to their lands, with one specific exception. By the terms of section 11 of the bill, the Oregon

City Claim (i. e., Dr. McLoughlin's land) was to be put
at the disposal of the Legislative Assembly for the establishment of a University. It was further provided
that Abernethy Island and such lots in Oregon City
as were held by any one except Dr. John McLoughlin
should be secured to the respective holders. The effect
of this section of the bill was simply to confiscate by
act of Congress all of McLoughlin's claim, amounting
to nearly six hundred and forty acres, including the site
of Oregon City. All persons who had secured pieces
of land from McLoughlin, previous to March 4, 1849,
whether fraudulently, e. g., the Abernethy Island, or by
purchase, were to be confirmed in their title. To secure
the passage of a bill containing such an iniquitous provision required more than ordinary duplicity. Thurston came to the task fully prepared to carry out the
behests of those to whom he must look for re-election.
To compass his ends he issued a letter to the members
of the House of Representatives concerning the proposed bill, and in particular, concerning section 11. The
part of the letter devoted to the discussion of McLoughlin's claim is a tissue of deliberate falsehoods. Among
other misstatements, Thurston declared: "This claim
has been wrongfully wrested by Dr. McLoughlin from
American citizens. The Methodist Mission first took
the claim, with the view of establishing here their mills
and missions. They were forced to leave it under the
fear of having the savages of Oregon let loose upon

them; and, successively, a number of citizens of our country have been driven from it while Dr. McLoughlin was yet at the head of the Hudson's Bay Company, west of the Rocky Mountains. Having at his command the Indians of the country, he has held it by violence and dint of threats up to this time." Again: "He (McLoughlin) is still an Englishman, still connected in interests with the Hudson's Bay Company, and still refuses to file his intention to become an American citizen."

3. Thurston's Calumnies.

McLoughlin had declared his intention of becoming an American citizen on May 30th of the previous year and had voted at the general election in June against Thurston, as Thurston was well aware. The calumny that McLoughlin had wrongfully wrested the claim from American citizens was so outrageous that Thurston thought it best to keep his letter to the Representatives from becoming known in Oregon until after the passage of the bill. The only copy of the letter that reached Oregon before that date bore on the reverse side in Thurston's handwriting the following note:

"Keep this still till next mail, when I shall send them generally. The debate on the California bill closes next Tuesday, when I hope to get it passed — my land bill; keep dark till next mail.

"June 9, 1850."   "THURSTON."

No wonder he wished the proceedings to be kept in the dark. They would not bear the light.

In the debate on the bill, Thurston declared that the Hudson's Bay Company had been waging war on our country for forty years. He continued: "Dr. McLoughlin has been their chief fugleman, first to cheat our government out of the whole country, and next to prevent its settlement. In 1845 he sent an express to Fort Hall, 800 miles, to warn American emigrants that if they attempted to come to Willamette they would all be cut off; they went and none were cut off. How, sir, would you reward Benedict Arnold, were he living? He fought the battle of the country, yet by one act of treason forfeited the respect of that country. A bill for his relief would fail, I am sure; yet this bill proposes to reward those who are now, have been, and ever will be more hostile to our country — more dangerous because more hidden, more jesuitical."

4. Friends and Enemies Pass Resolutions.

As soon as it became generally known that Thurston was resorting to falsehood and calumny to deprive Dr. McLoughlin of his land a public mass meeting of protest was held in Oregon City. A resolution was drafted repudiating the selection of McLoughlin's property for a university reservation, declaring McLoughlin "merits the gratitude of multitudes of persons in Oregon for the timely and long continued assistance rendered by

him in the settlement of the territory." A memorial was
sent to Congress setting forth that McLoughlin was
justly entitled to his land claim. But the bill had become a law before the memorial reached Washington
and the attention of Congress was being devoted to
more important concerns than the property rights of
an old man in the wilds of Oregon. Shortly after the
passage of the bill a mass meeting was held at Salem,
the stronghold of the Mission Party. Resolutions were
drawn up strongly upholding the action of Thurston;
declaring that "the Hudson's Bay Company, with Dr.
McLoughlin as their chief fugleman, have used every
means that could be invented by avarice, duplicity, cun-
ning and deception to retard American settlement, and
cripple the growth of American interests in Oregon."
And the framers of this resolution were the men whom
Dr. McLoughlin had fed and clothed and housed. He
had cared for their families and nursed their sick. He
had loaned them thousands of dollars. He had saved
them from the cruelty of the Indians. And this was
their expression of gratitude!

5. Last Years of McLoughlin.

In 1854 the lower house of the Oregon Legislature
refused to memorialize Congress in favor of the resti-
tution of McLoughlin's claim to its rightful owner, and
even a resolution expressing the gratitude of Oregon
for McLoughlin's work was indefinitely postponed.

And so the father and benefactor of Oregon had his lands confiscated, his extensive improvements rendered useless and unsalable, his very home taken from him by the iniquitous conspiracy. He was indeed suffered to occupy the house simply because no one had any interest in evicting him. It was no longer his. In a document already referred to, Dr. McLoughlin thus sums up the results of his labors in the Oregon Country: "I founded this settlement and prevented a war between the United States and Great Britain, and for doing this peaceably and quietly, I was treated by the British in such a manner that from self-respect I resigned my situation in the Hudson's Bay Company's service, . . . and the 'Oregon Land Bill' shows the treatment I received from the Americans." Fortified by the last rites of the Church, Dr. McLoughlin died in Oregon City, September 3, 1857, a broken-hearted man. He was buried in the Catholic churchyard. The church building has since been extended to cover the grave.

6. Tribute to the Memory of McLoughlin.

In October, 1862, three years after Oregon had become a State, the Legislative Assembly did tardy justice to the memory of McLoughlin by returning to his heirs, for the nominal figure of one thousand dollars, confiscated land claim. Twelve years had elapsed since the passage of the Oregon Donation Land Act reduced him to destitution, and five years had flown since his

body had been laid in the churchyard. Dr. John
McLoughlin was beyond power of legislative enact-
ments, but the State of Oregon did credit to itself by
this official condemnation of the conspiracy against its
greatest benefactor. Still no appropriate recognition
of McLoughlin has yet been shown by the Oregon country. In 1887 the people of Portland had a life-sized
portrait of McLoughlin painted for the Oregon Pioneer Association. The portrait hung in the place of
honor in the Senate chamber of the state capitol at
Salem, where it remained until the building was destroyed by fire a few years ago. In St. John's Catholic
Church, at Oregon City, is to be seen a memorial window representing McLoughlin as a knight of St. Gregory. The most fitting monument yet erected to his
memory is the parish school, at Oregon City, named
in his honor the "McLoughlin Institute," which was
dedicated with fitting ceremonies and addresses on Sunday, October 6, 1907.

The Catholics of the Pacific Northwest may claim
as their own the "Father of Oregon," they have a hero
that is found without blemish. "Of all the men," says
Mr. Holman, in the concluding paragraph of his *Life
of McLoughlin,* "whose lives and deeds are essential
parts of the history of the Oregon Country, Dr. John
McLoughlin stands supremely first — there is no second. In contemplating him all others sink into com-

parative insignificance. You may search the world over, and all its histories from the beginning of civilization to today, and you will find no nobler, no grander man than Dr. John McLoughlin. His life and character illustrate the kinship of man to God. He was God-like in his great fatherhood, in his great strength, in his great power, and in the exercise of his strength and of his power; he was Christ-like in his gentleness, in his tenderness, in his loving kindness, and in his humanity."

CHAPTER THIRTEEN

THE FIRST CATHOLIC SCHOOLS IN OREGON

1. St. Joseph's College Founded.

One of the earliest cares of Father Blanchet was the
establishment of schools for the children committed to
his pastoral solicitude. A wealthy French gentleman,
Joseph Larocque, made it possible to open a college for
boys at St. Paul. Larocque, whose home was in Paris,
had at an early date been heavily interested in the
Northwest Company, and after the amalgamation of
that Company with the Hudson's Bay Company in
1821, became chief trader in the latter company. He
donated 4,800 francs to Father Blanchet for the erection of a school. Work was begun in 1842 and the
school opened in the fall of 1843 under the name of
"St. Joseph's College," in honor of its generous founder.
On October 17 the college was blessed with solemn
ceremony in the presence of a large concourse of people. Father Langlois was placed in charge. On the
first day thirty boys entered as boarders, chiefly metis,

sons of farmers except one Indian boy who was the son of a chief. Some distance from the college there was in process of erection a convent for Sisters. In October of the same year Father Blanchet accompanied Dr. McLoughlin to Oregon City and selected a block for a Catholic Church — the site of the present St. John's Church and McLoughlin Institute, Oregon City. Early in 1844 the first pastor of Oregon City was appointed in the person of Father Demers, who celebrated Mass there for the first time on Sunday, March 3, of that year.

2. Sisters of Notre Dame Arrive.

A second reinforcement for the Catholic missions came early in August when Father DeSmet returned from Europe accompanied by four priests of the Society and by six Sisters of Notre Dame de Namur. These were Sisters Ignatius of Loyola, Cornelia, Aloysia, Albine, Norbertine and Catherine.

Father DeSmet at once established the Jesuit mission of St. Francis Xavier on a site secured for that purpose by the Vicar General. The Sisters of Notre Dame also took possession of the convent which was under construction in preparation for their arrival, but which, unfortunately, owing to the scarcity of mechanics, was still wanting in doors and sashes. The Sisters were soon initiated into the requirements of pioneer life. One might be seen handling the plane, another glazing, and still others painting the windows and doors. More than thirty children of the Canadian farmers were quickly enrolled in the new Academy. The Sisters entered their new convent early in the month of October and a few days later their humble chapel was solemnly consecrated by Father Blanchet. So immediate was the success of the Sisters that Father DeSmet, writing under date of October 9, 1844, says that another foundation was projected at "Cuhute" (Oregon City), where the Sisters opened their second school in Oregon in the fall of 1848.

In a postscript to the letter above mentioned, Father DeSmet writes as follows: "On the 9th of September the good Sisters commenced instructing women and children who were preparing for their First Communion. As their house was not yet habitable they were obliged to give their instructions in the open air. In three days' time they had already nineteen pupils from sixteen to sixty years of age, all of whom came from a distance bringing with them provisions for several days and sleeping in the woods, exposed to all the inclemencies of the weather. It is easy to conceive by this how eager these poor people are for instruction." Later, Father DeSmet writes that the Sisters are anxious for the completion of their new home as they were promised thirty Canadian pupils whose tuition would enable the Sisters to give gratuitous support and protection to the hapless orphans of the forest. He gives what he terms "the brilliant prospectus" of the Academy, in which he sets forth the quarterly tuition charges in terms of flour, meat, potatoes, eggs, salt, candles, tea and rice. Notwithstanding this crude and primitive method of collecting tuition Father DeSmet was impressed with the bright prospects for the future.

3. Captain Bailey Visits St. Paul.

We learn something of the internal affairs of the boys' school from letters of the Sisters. In July, 1844, Captain Bailey of the British frigate Modeste, accompanied by two officers, came to St. Paul and assisted at services on Sunday in the chapel. The children from the college and from the parish were arranged in two rows in the sanctuary. The British captain was much impressed by the excellent discipline which the pupils manifested. A public examination at which he assisted was held at the college in French and English, writing and arithmetic. The following summer we read that Vicar General Demers came to examine the pupils of the Academy before the distribution of prizes, and gave a talk to the parents on their duties.

4. Spiritual Exercises at the Academy.

The spiritual exercises of the Sisters possess an interest of their own. On November 7, 1844, they entered on an eight-day retreat with Father DeVos as Director. This was the first religious retreat in the

Oregon Country. The Forty Hours' devotion was held for the first time at the Feast of the Epiphany, January 6, 1845, just six years after the blessing of the church. On October 2, 1845, the children were enrolled in the scapular and two of them consecrated to St. Agnes, marking the beginning of a Sodality. Not to be omitted is a reference to a miraculous statue of our Lady of Seven Dolors, a gift of the "Orphelines" of Lima, Peru. Its shrine stood in a secluded corner of the grounds. A beginning of domestic science is noted in that the children are taught to make their own clothing, and some who had attained greater efficiency were engaged in embroidering a rochet for the Archbishop on his return.

5. Idyllic Life at St. Paul.

It was of this period that an old pioneer writes as follows concerning the settlement at St. Paul: "There was a time when French Prairie was the home spot of the Pacific Northwest, when the Americans had not yet gone into rendezvous on the Missouri border and had not taught their prairie schooners the long way across the plains. In those ante-pioneer days the Candian French had made their homes on the beautiful prairie and in the absence of their country-women had espoused the dusky maidens of the Calapooias, who raised for them bright-eyed groups of half-breed boys and girls. The Catholic Fathers were here to bless the union and guide the lives of these youths, and the condition of these people was one of peace and plenty. The earliest comers among the Americans took homes among them and speak with pleasant memories of the quiet, peaceful, faraway life which the French and half-breed population enjoyed. These remember seeing the young people assemble on the Sabbath where is now the Catholic Church of St. Paul and the pictures they draw are charmingly illustrative of the idyllic period that Oregon passed through and the quiet pastoral lives these Canadians lived."

6. Father Blanchet Acts as Judge.

Duflot de Mofras, who visited Oregon in 1844 and spent some days with the Vicar General at St. Paul, recounts how Father Blanchet acted as judge over his flock. A French-Canadian was accused of stealing a horse from an American. An exhibition of patriarchal justice was given. The fathers of all the families were assembled. The case was tried, and the culprit found guilty. Father Blanchet rendered judgment that the thief should restore the horse and should remain at the door of the church for three months during services. The decision, adds Mofras, was accepted without question. (Vol. II, page 218.)

The return of the Archbishop in 1847 brought to the Sisters of Notre Dame a reinforcement in the persons of Sister Renilda and her companions, which enabled them in pursuance of the plan already mentioned to open a school at Oregon City on September 12, 1848. The Archbishop, too, late in the month of December, transferred his residence to Oregon City, the official seat of his vast diocese.

7. Sudden Closing of the Schools.

The year 1849 was to open a series of misfortunes for the Church in Oregon. Gold had been discovered in California and a large emigration of families from French Prairie for the mines took place in May. As a consequence, St. Joseph's College for boys, which had been founded in 1844, was closed in June, 1849, and never reopened its doors. The consequence of the emigration from St. Paul was the subsequent closing of the Jesuit Mission of St. Francis Xavier on the Willamette, and the withdrawal of the Fathers of that Society from mission work in Oregon. The Sisters of Notre Dame were forced by the same circumstances to abandon their school at St. Paul in 1852. Meanwhile a similar misfortune had overtaken Oregon City. It will be recalled that by the terms of the Oregon Donation Land Act of 1849, the Oregon City claim was appropriated by the state. As a result of this act no land could be sold in Oregon City and the town rapidly declined. Hence in 1853 the Sisters of Notre Dame were led to close their remaining school at the Falls of the Willamette, and the Archdiocese was bereft at once of all its religious and of its educational institutions.

HON. PETER H. BURNETT
FIRST CHIEF JUSTICE OF OREGON AND
FIRST GOVERNOR OF CALIFORNIA

CHAPTER FOURTEEN

ESTABLISHMENT OF THE HIERARCHY

Establishment of Ecclesiastical Province. — Secures
Recruits and Aid in Europe. — The Archbishop Re-
turns to Oregon. — Activity of Vicar-General Demers.
— First Ordination in Oregon.—Arrival of the Bishop
of Walla Walla. — Consecration of Bishop Demers. —
Early Life of Burnett. — Reads the Campbell-Purcell
Debate. — Received into the Church

I. Establishment of Ecclesiastical Province.

Immediately after his consecration in Montreal as
Titular Bishop of Drasa, Bishop Blanchet decided to
go to Europe before returning to his Vicariate. His
purpose was to obtain from Rome assistant bishops for
the vast territory under his jurisdiction, to secure new
missionaries and more Sisters and to collect funds to
enable him to build the churches and schools which
he saw to be necessary in the immediate future. This
task occupied him from October, 1845, to October,
1846. He first visited Belgium in order to secure a
reinforcement of the Sisters of Notre Dame de Namur.
It will be recalled that six Sisters of this community
had accompanied Father DeSmet to Oregon in 1844.
He was successful in getting the promise of seven addi-

tional Sisters. The Bishop then visited the principal cities of Belgium and everywhere aroused the greatest interest in his mission. He next turned his steps towards the Eternal City, spending Christmas at Marseilles and reaching Rome January 5, 1846. He obtained an audience with Pope Gregory XVI and was subsequently received several times by His Holiness. Acting upon the advice of influential friends in Rome he decided to request of the Holy See the establishment of an ecclesiastical province with an archbishop and several suffragans. To this end he presented to the Congregation of the Propaganda an extended memorial dealing with the history and conditions and needs of his vast Vicariate. The result of his petition was that by Briefs dated July 2, 1846, the Vicariate was erected into an ecclesiastical province with the three Sees of Oregon City, Walla Walla and Vancouver Island. Five other districts were also named in the Briefs, namely: Fort Hall, Fort Colville, New Caledonia, Nesqually and Princess Charlotte Island, but these were associated in administration, with the three already mentioned. Bishop Blanchet was promoted to the position of Archbishop of Oregon City and Father Demers to that of Bishop of Vancouver Island, while a brother of the new Archbishop, the Reverend A. M. A. Blanchet, Canon of the Montreal Cathedral, was selected as Bishop of Walla Walla.

2. Secures Recruits and Aid in Europe.

Bishop Blanchet remained in Rome four months, visiting with all the delight of a pious pilgrim the great basilicas and churches of the Holy City and the other monuments of Christian antiquity. The catacombs were an object of his special devotion, and before leaving Rome he obtained relics of Sts. Jovian, Severin, Flavia and Victoria. On his return to Oregon these relics were distributed as special gifts to various churches and institutions, where they are still preserved. Leaving Rome on May 8 the Bishop returned to France by way of Genoa and Marseilles. He visited some days at Avignon and spent a week as guest at the Grand Seminary of Lyons. Here he addressed the three hundred seminarians and secured three of them for the Oregon Mission. These were B. Delorme, afterwards Vicar General of Oregon City, and the author of an extended heroic poem entitled *L'Homme-Dieu.;* J. F. Jayol and F. Veyret. Bishop Blanchet now visited Prussia, Bavaria and Austria. Leaving Paris in the middle of June he visited Aix-La-Chapelle and Cologne, and then ascending the Rhine stopped at Bonn and Mayence and other of the Rhine cities, finally reaching Munich, where he spent a week as a guest of the discalced Fathers of St. Augustine. Descending the Danube he remained for three weeks a guest of the Redemptorist Fathers at Vienna. It was not until his return to Paris, however, that he learned of the successful termination of his representations in Rome and his promotion to the Metropolitan See of Oregon City.

In his long journey he was everywhere met with the warm sympathy of the highest authorities in Church and State. He was received in audience by the King and Queen of Belgium, by the King of Bavaria, by the Emperor and Empress of Austria, and three times by Louis Philippe, King of France. The last named sovereign secured for him a gift amounting to nearly eighteen thousand francs for the Oregon Mission. He received many other valuable gifts, and the railroads of Belgium and France gave many favors to his party.

3. The Archbishop Returns to Oregon.

It was not until February 22, 1847, that the Archbishop set sail for Oregon from Brest with his company in the *L'Etoile du Matin*. He brought with him twenty-one persons for the Oregon Mission. These were seven Sisters of Notre Dame de Namur, three Jesuit Fathers and three Brothers of the Society, five secular priests, namely, Le Bas, McCormick, Deleveau, Pretot and Veyret, two deacons, B. Delorme and J. F. Jayol, and a student, T. Mesplie. After a journey of nearly six months the L'Etoile du Matin reached the mouth of the Willamette River, and the party disembarked on August 19, 1847. On August 25 the Archbishop reached his new Cathedral at Oregon City and celebrated Mass there the following day. He proceeded thence to his old missionary field at St. Paul and robed in the episcopal vestments chanted the Te Deum in thanksgiving for his happy return and gave benediction of the Blessed Sacrament to the large concourse of Catholics and non-Catholics who gathered to greet him.

4. Activity of Vicar General Demers.

During the absence of Archbishop Blanchet in 1845-6 the Church in Oregon was administered by Vicar General Demers. Father De Vos was stationed at Oregon City and was in charge of Vancouver, and Father Accolti, S. J., Superior of the Jesuit Mission at St. Paul. Father Bolduc remained in charge of St. Joseph's College. Great building activity was manifested at St. Paul at this time. St. Joseph's College was enlarged. A new chapel was in course of construction for the Sisters, who had more than forty children in their school. The cornerstone of a new brick church (the first brick church in Oregon) was blessed by Father Demers on May 26, 1846, and the church was dedicated on November 1 of the same year. Meanwhile Father Vercruisse had constructed a church at St. Louis. The new Church at Oregon City, which was destined to be the Cathedral, had been blessed and opened for divine worship on February 8, 1846. Here the efforts of Father De Vos met with great success and his zeal was crowned by the reception of a number of distinguished converts, among whom were Dr. J. E. Long, Secretary of the Provisional Government, and Peter H. Burnett, Chief Justice of Oregon.

5. First Ordination in Oregon.

On Sunday, September 12, the Archbishop administered the sacrament of Confirmation at St. Paul and on the following Sunday raised Mr. Jayol to the priesthood, this being the first ordination in the Oregon Country. The Archbishop revisited his missions at Fort Vancouver and the St. Francis Xavier mission at Cowlitz, administering confirmation in each place. On October 31 he was back at St. Paul and ordained the future Vicar General Delorme to the priesthood.

6. Arrival of the Bishop of Walla Walla.

Right Rev. A. M. Blanchet, who had been consecrated Bishop of Walla Walla in Montreal on September 27, 1846, arrived on September 5 at Fort Walla Walla after a long journey of five months in wagons across the plains by way of St. Louis. The Bishop of Walla Walla was accompanied by four Oblate Fathers of Marseilles and Father Brouillet, as Vicar General, and also Father Rousseau and William Leclaire, deacon. The Bishop and his party were received very cordially by Mr. McBean, commandant of the Fort, who with his family were Catholics and who figured in the Whitman disaster which was then imminent. The

Bishop of Walla Walla established his mission a short distance from the mission of Dr. Whitman, among the Umatilla Indians at Wailatpu.

7. Consecration of Bishop Demers.

While the new episcopal See was thus being established at Walla Walla, Archbishop Blanchet was preparing to consecrate the Bishop-elect of Vancouver Island. To this dignity had been called Father Demers, the companion of Father Blanchet in the first missionary labors in Oregon. The rejoicing with which the Archbishop's return was greeted culminated on the Feast of St. Andrew, November 30, 1847, in the consecration of Bishop-elect Demers, at St. Paul, in the presence of numerous clergy and a large concourse of the faithful. The outlook for the new ecclesiastical province was bright and as the pioneer Bishops looked over the field which they had so toilfully entered nine years earlier there seemed to be promise on every hand of a bountiful harvest to crown their labors.

8. Early Life of Burnett.

Among the most notable of the Oregon pioneers was Peter H. Burnett, first Chief Justice of Oregon and later first Governor of California. The following account of his life is furnished by himself. He was born of Baptist parents in 1808, but grew up without belief in Christianity. In 1840 he joined the Disciples or

Campbellites. He was one of the prominent leaders of the great emigration of 1843 and was afterwards prominently identified with the provisional government of Oregon in a legal capacity. Of his conversion he writes as follows: "While I was temporarily located at Fort Vancouver I attended High Mass as a mere spectator on Christmas at midnight (1843). I had never witnessed anything like it before, and the profound solemnity of the services, the intense yet calm fervor of the worshipers, the great and marked difference between the two forms of worship, and the instantaneous reflection that this was the church claiming to be the only true church did make the deepest impression on me for the moment. In all my religious experience I had never felt an impulse so profound, so touching. But as I knew nothing of the reasons upon which the Catholic theory assumes to rest, I soon thought I saw errors that I could not sanction. And then there came a painful revulsion in my feeling. . . .

9. Reads the Campbell-Purcell Debate.

"My knowledge of the Catholic theory was exceedingly general and indefinite. I had never read a work in its favor, and had never heard but two Catholic sermons and they were not on controversial points. In the fall of 1844 a Baptist preacher settled in my immediate neighborhood who had the published debate between

Campbell and Purcell. I borrowed and read the book. But while the attentive reading of the debate did not convince me of the entire truth of the Catholic theory, I was greatly astonished to find that so much could be said in its support. On many points and those of great importance it was clear to my mind that Mr. Campbell had been overthrown. I arose from the reading of that discussion still a Protestant. . . .

"My mind was, therefore, left in a state of restless uncertainty; and I determined to examine the question between Catholics and Protestants thoroughly. I procured all the works on both sides within my reach. The investigation occupied all my spare time for about eighteen months. I examined carefully, prayerfully and earnestly until I was satisfied beyond a doubt that the old church was the true and the only true church." (*The Path Which Led a Protestant Lawyer to the Catholic Church,* Preface.)

10. Received into the Church

"After an impartial and calm investigation, I became convinced of the truth of the Catholic theory and went to Oregon City in June, 1846, to join the Old Church. There I found the heroic and saintly Father De Vos, who had spent one or more years among the Flathead Indians. He received me into the church." (*Recollections of an Old Pioneer,* page 189.)

CHAPTER FIFTEEN

THE WHITMAN MASSACRE AND LEGEND

1. Whitman Founds Mission Among Cayuse.

Two days before the consecration of Bishop Demers, a catastrophe occurred in Eastern Oregon which
brought the Catholic missions in Oregon to the brink
of ruin. We refer to the savage massacre of Dr. Whitman and his wife at the Wailatpu Mission. A word
of explanation is necessary to understand the consequences of this event. As early as 1836, Dr. Whitman
had taken up his residence among the Cayuse Indians
as representative of the American Board Mission. Here
he acted as general manager of this mission and as
medical adviser to the savages. For a time his work
seemed to progress very satisfactorily and the mission
exerted considerable influence among the Indians. Soon,
however, the savages became suspicious of the encroachments of the whites on their lands, and their suspicions

were further aggravated by the fatal termination of an epidemic of measles which spread among them, and which Dr. Whitman attempted to cure. It was the custom among the Indians to kill the medicine man who failed to bring relief to the sick. A story, too, was spread by a half-breed named Joe Lewis, that Dr. Whitman was poisoning the Indians to get possession of their lands. This, taken in connection with the jealous nature of the Indians and the aggression of the whites, fanned the flame into a fierce blaze of indignation against the head of the mission, and they resolved upon the death of Dr. Whitman. Meanwhile the quarrels of the various members of the mission, especially those of Spalding and Whitman and Mr. Gray, had brought the mission to the very verge of destruction by causing the order of the Board in February, 1842, for the discontinuance of three of its four stations and the recalling to the States of Gray and Spalding. Whitman's ride was made for the purpose of securing, and it did secure, the rescission of this destructive order.

2. The Massacre.

The decadence of this mission went on very rapidly after 1839 till it was destroyed by the dreadful massacre of November 29-December 8, 1847, in which Dr. and Mrs. Whitman and twelve others were slain, and fifty-three others, mostly women and children, were taken prisoners. (Marshall, Vol. II, page 38.) The following day Vicar General Brouillet, ignorant of what had occurred, came to the Cayuse camp to baptize some sick children. He arrived there late in the evening and learned of the atrocious outrage. The next morning he went to the place of the massacre and buried the bodies of the dead in the presence of the murderers. Leaving the scene of the massacre, he hastened away to warn Mr. Spalding, the mission minister, of the danger. He was accompanied, much against his will, by one of the Cayuse Indians. He met the minister three miles from the camp. He pleaded with the Indian to spare the life of Spalding. The Indian replied that he could not take the responsibility of doing so himself, but would return to camp to consult the others. When the Indian had gone, Father Brouillet informed Spalding of the massacre, and giving him his own supply of food, urged him for his safety to leave the neighborhood at once. Mr. Spalding took to flight, and the Vicar General continued his way and had scarcely gone a few miles until he was overtaken by the savages in search of Mr. Spalding. A few days later Bishop Blanchet of Walla Walla, assembled the Indian chiefs and expressed his concern at the outrage, and urged them to save the widows and orphans. As soon as tidings of the massacre reached Fort Vancouver, Chief Factor Ogden started without delay to rescue the captives. He reached Fort Walla Walla on December 19, and assembled all of the Indian chiefs on December 23, demanding from them all of their prisoners and promising to use his influence to prevent war. On December 29, Ogden returned to Fort Walla Walla with the prisoners.

3. Spalding's Ingratitude.

No sooner had Mr. Spalding reached a place of safety, under the protection of Mr. Ogden, than he began a systematic vilification of Bishop Blanchet and Father Brouillet. Forgetting all sentiments of gratitude, he accused the Bishop and his clergy of instigating the horrible massacre. So outrageous were these accusations that they aroused the deepest and intensest prejudice against the Bishop and the Catholic Church generally, and the excitement became so great that the American volunteers in leaving the Willamette Valley in pursuit of the Indians said that their first shots would be for the Bishop and his priests. For several months feeling ran so high that the Catholic churches and institutions were in danger of being burned down. As a matter of fact the leaders of the massacre were members of their own mission as is confessed in the following letter of Rev. H. H. Spalding to Rev. D. Greene, under date of January 24, 1848. (Marshall, Vol. II, page 204.)

"Most of these murderers were from the camp of Joseph who, you will recollect, was one of the first two received into our church and who up to this event, has sustained a good Christian character." Another offender was "Hezekiah the principal Cayuse chief, and one often mentioned in my letters as one of our most diligent scholars, three winters in our school at Clear Water and a member of our church."

4. Causes of the Whitman Massacre.

The particular causes of the Whitman massacre have been well stated by Marshall, as follows:

1. The folly of Gray in starting with several Indians to the States in 1837. The Indians were all killed.

2. The murder of Elijah Hedding, the son of a Walla Walla chief, at Sutter's Fort in California.

3. The acts and words of Tom Hill, the Delaware or Shoshone Indian who had been educated at Dartmouth College, and who embittered the savages against the whites.

4. The failure of the Indians to get property from the missionaries in payment for the use of the land occupied by the mission stations.

5. Their anger at the constantly increasing throng of whites going through their country to settle in the Willamette Valley.

6. The belief of the Indians that the missionaries were growing rich from the produce of their lands.

7. The belief of the Indians that Whitman was poisoning them, confirmed to their ignorant and super-

stitious minds by the exceedingly careless way in which strychnine was used at the various stations of the Mission.

8. The deadly epidemic of measles, complicated with dysentery, which was communicated to the Indians by the migration of 1847.

9. The terrible severity of the winter of 1846-7, which rendered the Indians much more susceptible than usual to the ravages of the diseases which swept off so large a part of the Cayuse and Walla Wallas in the autumn of 1847.

10. Whitman's unwisdom in continuing to doctor among them as if they were civilized people, in spite of numerous threats by Indians from as early as 1837 that they would kill him if he failed to cure them, and although he knew well that from his first arrival in the country, he had among them the reputation of a great sorcerer or "medicine man," and although he equally well knew that it was a very common practice among the Indians to kill their own medicine men when they failed to cure their patients.

5. Anti-Catholic Prejudice.

The excitement due to the murder of Dr. Whitman and the subsequent Cayuse War had subsided and the public mind was restored to quiet when a new incident arose, in July, 1848, which aroused the prejudice against the Catholics to a higher pitch than before. This was the interception at The Dalles by Lieutenant Rodgers of ammunition which was being taken to the Rocky Mountain missions conducted by the Jesuit Fathers. Those missions were dependent largely upon hunting, and each summer the Fathers in charge imported a stock of powder and balls for the winter's use. Lieutenant Rodgers reported that these arms and ammunition were to be distributed among the Indians of the interior for the extermination of the Protestants. The state of the popular mind may be imagined when such a story would receive credence and become the source of a general anti-Catholic movement. In December, 1848, a petition was introduced into Territorial Legislature for the expulsion of the Catholic clergy from Oregon. More sober counsel prevailed, however, and the petition was lost. But the work of the Catholic missionaries in Eastern Oregon was frustrated for two decades, and even in the Willamette Valley it was retarded.

6. The Whitman Myth.

The influence of the Whitman story was, however, not to rest here. Mr. Spalding, in order to discredit the work of the Catholic missionaries, invented an heroic narrative of Whitman's service to Oregon, in which the Catholic clergy were held up to public view as the enemies of American domination. While this narrative belongs chronologically to a period of history nearly twenty years subsequent to the Whitman massacre, it will be best for us to give an account of the matter in this place.

7. Earliest Version.

The earliest published version of the Whitman story is the brief and vague one written by S. A. Clarke, which appeared in the *Sacramento Union* of November 16, 1864. The story is to be found in two very variant forms in two letters to the American Board written by Rev. George H. Atkinson, November 20, 1858, and September 7, 1859. These are doubtless the earliest written forms of the legend. The most generally accepted version of the story is that published by Rev. H. H. Spalding in the *Pacific,* the California organ of the Congregationalists, October 19 and November 9, 1865. The story of how Whitman saved Oregon to the United States, according to the narrative of Spalding and Gray, is as follows:

8. The Dinner at Fort Walla Walla.

"In September, 1842, Dr. Whitman was called to visit a patient at Fort Walla Walla. While there he took dinner with the traders and clerks of the Hudson's Bay Company, who were on their way to New Caledonia. While they were at dinner, word arrived that an emigration from Red River had passed the Rocky Mountains and was near Fort Colville. An exclamation of joy burst from the whole table, at first unaccountable to Dr. Whitman, till a young priest, not thinking there was an American at the table, sprang to his feet and swinging his hands in the air exclaimed, 'Hurrah for for Columbia! (Oregon), America is too late! We have the country.' In an instant, Dr. Whitman, as by instinct, saw through the whole plan. He immediately arose from the table, asked to be excused, sprang upon his horse, rode to his mission, and without stopping to dismount, told his co-workers: 'I am going to cross the Rocky Mountains and reach Washington this winter and bring an emigration over the mountains next spring, or this country is lost.'

9. How Oregon Was Saved.

"Leaving his missionary associates, he entered upon his famous ride, and reached Washington the last of March, 1843. There he sought an interview with Secretary Webster, and laid before him the great importance of Oregon to the United States; but he found Webster on the point of trading off Oregon to Great Britain for a cod-fishery on the Banks of Newfoundland. Whitman then had an interview with President Tyler, who promised that Oregon should not be traded off provided Dr. Whitman should establish a wagon route through the mountains to the Columbia River. Whitman thereupon organized a caravan of nearly 200 wagons with a great emigration, leaving Missouri on the last of April and emerging on the plains of the

Columbia on the 4th of September, 1843. Thus was Oregon saved to the Union and the nefarious plans of the Catholic missionaries frustrated by Whitman's heroism."

10. False in Every Important Detail.

Such is the thrilling story of Whitman's services, which was published to the world by Spalding for the first time in 1865, seventeen years after the death of Marcus Whitman. Of this story we have only to remark that it is false in every important particular, as the following points will indicate:

1. There is no emigration from the Red River reaching Oregon in 1842.

2. There was no young priest in Eastern Oregon in September, 1842.

3. Whitman's journey was undertaken, not to save Oregon, but to save his own mission from being closed down by the order which had come from the Board in the East; and this journey was planned and authorized by his associates in missionary work, as is shown by the authoritative documents of the mission.

4. The story concerning Webster is too puerile to deserve notice. Every administration from 1814 down to 1846 had insisted on nothing south of forty-nine degrees as "our ultimatum" for the northern boundary of Oregon. Webster positively declared in January and

February, 1843, "that he had never made nor entertained nor meditated any proposition to accept of the Columbia River, or any other line south of the forty-ninth degree, as a negotiable boundary line for the United States." (Marshall, Vol. II, page 192.)

5. Whitman had nothing to do with organizing the emigration of 1843, but fell in with it after it was organized, and accompanied it to Oregon.

The Whitman story, however, in spite of its purely mythical character, found its way into encyclopedias and general histories and chronicles of Oregon, and especially through Barrows' *History of Oregon,* which was published in 1884, the story received universal dissemination.

11. Non-Catholic Historians Demolish Legend.

The final disposal of the myth must be credited to two non-Catholic historians, Prof. Edward Gaylord Bourne, of Yale, and Mr. W. I. Marshall, of Chicago. The former, in his *Essays in Historical Criticism,* has dissected the Whitman legend; the latter, in his two volumes on the *Acquisition of Oregon,* and *the Long-Suppressed Evidence Concerning Marcus Whitman,* has finally demolished the story and exposed the animus of those who built it up.

"It is evident," says Marshall, "to any one who will study the origin and development of the Whitman legend that it would never have been heard of, had the National Government paid the thirty or forty thousand dollars claimed by Spalding and Eels for the destruction of the mission, and allowed their claims for a mile square of land around each mission station. . . . This makes the origin of the legend vastly more sordid than I had previously supposed." (Vol. II, page 51.)

Notes to This Chapter, by Mr. Clinton A. Snowden.

(a) "The President and his Cabinet had received a special report from Commodore Wilkes more than eight months before Whitman reached Washington giving vastly more information in regard to the value of Oregon than Whitman possessed."

(b) "Professor McMaster in his *History of the People of the United States,* shows that the people of the Western States, particularly, were fully aware of the value of the Oregon country, and that public meetings had been held in various places, and a National Convention had been called to meet at Cincinnati to urge Congress to hasten settlement of the boundary question, before Whitman reached any frontier settlement on his way East."

CHAPTER SIXTEEN

A DECADE OF STRUGGLE (1848-1858)

First Provincial Council is Held. — Bishop Demers
Reaches Vancouver Island. — Diocese of Nesqually
Created. — Conditions Serious at Oregon City. —
State of the Diocese in 1852. — Archbishop Tours
South America for Aid. — A Discouraging Outlook

1. First Provincial Council Is Held.

Notwithstanding the unfortunate events which
broke up the Catholic missions among the Indians in
Eastern Oregon, Archbishop Blanchet opened the first
Provincial Council of Oregon in the archiepiscopal residence at St. Paul on February 28, 1848. Indeed the
assembling of the bishops of the province was due to
the Whitman massacre which caused the closing of the
mission at Walla Walla and threw the Bishop temporarily upon the charity and hospitality of the Archbishop. Bishop Demers, who had been consecrated on
the 30th of the preceding November, was still at St.
Paul. It was an unexpected opportunity for them to
deliberate on the needs of their various dioceses before
again separating. The three sessions of the council
were held with all solemnity. Disciplinary regulations

were enacted for the province and decrees formulated which afterwards received the approbation of the Holy See.

2. Bishop Demers Reaches Vancouver Island.

Immediately after the council had dissolved, Bishop Demers set out for Europe by way of Canada to secure co-workers for the diocese of Vancouver Island, having at that time not even one priest for the vast territory placed under his care. It was not until August 20, 1852, that he returned to take possession of his See. In a letter dated Victoria, October 26, 1852, he tells of his journey and the difficulties attending it. The missionaries whom he had secured in Europe came by sea in two sailing vessels which carried French immigrants to California. The Bishop himself came by way of Panama to San Francisco, where he found that two of his priests had arrived safely, but the second vessel with two other priests, a physician and two other lay attendants for the mission, had not arrived, being detained by mutiny on board at Rio de Janeiro. The Bishop proceeded to Vancouver Island with his two missionaries and found two others there (a priest and a sub-deacon) who had preceded him by four months. Arrived at his destination he was lodged in a little house which had been built by the Hudson's Bay Company for the use of Father Lamfrit, O. M. I., who had been sent to Victoria early in March, 1849. The Bishop tells us that on Sunday,

September 5, after vespers he took solemn possession of his diocese "plaudente populo cleroque!" On the 29th, another ceremony full of novelty and interest to his people (the savages) took place in the blessing of one of the bells which the Bishop had brought from London. It weighed fifty pounds. The following day the bell was suspended from a tower formed of the trunks of three trees. That evening (September 30) "the Bishop of Vancouver had the consolation of ringing the first Angelus that had ever been heard in the hills or valleys of Vancouver Island. Fourteen years had flown since I rang for the first time the Angelus at St. Francis Xavier on the Cowlitz." Years of toil and self-sacrifice among the Indians and the pioneer whites who formed his flock were again opening before the Bishop who had already borne the heats and burdens of the day as an humble missionary in Oregon. In 1853 the educational and missionary work of the diocese was strengthened by the arrival of the Sisters of St. Anne and the Oblate Fathers.

3. Diocese of Nesqually Created.

Meanwhile the Bishop of Walla Walla sought to return to his mission at Umatilla, having remained at Oregon City until after Easter Sunday, 1848. When he reached The Dalles he was forbidden by the Superintendent of Indian Affairs to go back among the Indians owing to the disturbed condition of the relations between the Indians and the whites. The Bishop established St. Peter's Mission at The Dalles, where he remained until the end of September, 1850. In response to a petition of the Provincial Council of 1848, there arrived from Rome briefs bearing the date of May 31, 1850, creating the district of Nesqually into a diocese and transferring the Bishop of Walla Walla to that See. The Diocese of Walla Walla was suppressed. In consequence of this order Bishop Blanchet, now Bishop of Nesqually quitted The Dalles and on October 27, 1850, took up his residence at Fort Vancouver.[1] The following year Bishop Blanchet went to Mexico to collect for the missions and churches of his diocese and returned with a successful collection of money, sacred vessels, pictures and sacerdotal vestments. He had previously appealed for assistance to the Archbishop of Quebec and we find in the pastoral letters of Archbishop Signay a recommendation of the work of Bishop Blanchet and the appointment of a collection to be taken up throughout the diocese for his benefit. Another source of aid to the necessitous diocese was the fund supplied by the Society for the Propagation of the Faith.

---

1. On June 29, 1853, at the recommendation of the First Plenary Council of Baltimore (1852), which Archbishop Blanchet and the Bishop of Nesqually attended, the Columbia River and parallel 46 became the line of division between the Dioceses of Oregon City and Nesqually from the Pacific Ocean to the Rocky Mountains. Fort Nesqually was never more than nominally the seat of the diocese. The Bishop resided at Fort Vancouver until Bishop O'Dea moved to Seattle. Since 1909 the title of the diocese has been Seattle.

4. Conditions Serious at Oregon City.

But hard as were conditions in the dioceses of Vancouver Island and Nesqually, they did not wear the serious aspect that they assumed in the Archdiocese of Oregon City. The building operations at St. Paul and Oregon City, which we chronicled in an earlier chapter, involved the archdiocese in very heavy debt. Had the community continued to grow normally, the required amount of money might possibly have been forthcoming, though it must be conceded that the new buildings, the church at St. Paul and the church and convent at Oregon City, were projected on a scale scarcely warranted by the most hopeful view of the situation. But whatever might have been the outcome under normal circumstances, the result was disastrous under the untoward conditions that arose. The discovery of gold in California was followed by an exodus of Catholic families from French Prairie, greatly crippling the resources of the chief parish in the archdiocese. The misfortune which overtook Oregon City when McLoughlin's claim was unjustly taken from him and appropriated for a university has already been mentioned (Chapter XII). Business was soon at a standstill, and after 1850, the population declined. The new school was deserted (see Chapter XIII, par. 7) and the congregation gradually dwindled away. Another misfortune overtook the Archbishop, when in 1849 a vessel, the Vancouver,

carrying the annual provision of merchandise for Fort
Vancouver, was shipwrecked at the mouth of the Columbia. The entire cargo was lost, including several
thousand dollars' worth of effects destined for the missions of the archdiocese.

5. State of the Diocese in 1852.

An interesting view of the state of the diocese in
1852 is to be had from the pen of St.-Amant, an envoy
of the French government who visited Oregon in that
year. St.-Amant spent some days with Archbishop Blanchet at Oregon City, and reports that "the archiepiscopal palace was worthy of John the Baptist." Speaking
of conditions at St. Paul he writes: "The priest is everything to the families on French Prairie — friend, con-
fidant, law-giver, counsellor, arbiter, judge. The financial condition is very unsatisfactory. The churches are
mortgaged to heretics and unless the Catholics make a
strenuous effort to save them, they will change altars
and lose the Real Presence"[1] (page 179). In the former
residence of the Archbishop at St. Paul, St.-Amant was
astonished to find five hundred volumes containing the
writings of the Fathers of the Church (Migne's Pa-
trology) in Latin and Greek. He observed that these

---

1. St.-Amant met McLoughlin at Oregon City. He speaks of
him in the following terms: "McLoughlin, an old man now, but very
straight and of superb bearing. Napoleon was always his idol. He
gives an example of extreme Catholic devotion and receives Communion on every occasion."

were scarcely the equipment to be expected in the home
of a missionary among the savages.

6. Archbishop Tours South America for Aid.

In order to meet the debts of the archdiocese, Archbishop Blanchet decided to tour South America for
financial assistance. He left Oregon City in the fall of
1855 with a letter of authorization from the Prefect
of the Congregation of Propaganda. He traversed several of the South American states, spending some time
in Peru and Bolivia. He was especially successful in
Chile, where he had published in 1856 in Spanish a
pamphlet giving a sketch of the Ecclesiastical Province
of Oregon. This sketch gives an account of the history
of Oregon exploration and missionary activity and contains an appeal of the Archbishop for aid in which he
presents a vivid picture of the multiplying misfortunes
which have befallen the diocese. The Archbishop returned in December, 1857, after two years' absence,
with a collection that enabled him to meet the debts
of the diocese.

7. A Discouraging Outlook.

The financial difficulties of the diocese were not
the only ones. The schools had all been closed; all the
religious, both men and women, had left the diocese;
the clergy diminished from 19 to 7; missions that were
once flourishing were now unattended; work among

the Indians was paralyzed; bigotry and prejudice were spreading apace, and the seat of the diocese, Oregon City, declining from day to day. The state of the diocese in 1855-56 is summed up in the following report: Oregon City, Cathedral of the Sacred Heart, Most Rev. F. N. Blanchet (absent) and Rev. Patrick Mackin; St. Paul, Marion County, Rev. Myles O'Reilly; St. Louis, Very Rev. B. Delorme, V. G., and Rev. A. Le Bas; Portland, Rev. Jas. Croke, who goes each summer to Southern Oregon, that is, Jacksonville, Scotsburgh, Winchester, Eugene City and other places; The Dalles, Rev. T. Mesplie. Total number of churches, six; clergy, seven. The years of 1855-56 may be taken as the nadir of the Catholic missions in Oregon.

CHAPTER SEVENTEEN

PORTLAND BECOMES A CATHOLIC CENTER

Father Croke, First Pastor of Portland.—The Church
Moved to New Location. — Catholic Census in 1855.
— The Archbishop Secures the Sisters of the Holy
Names. — St. Mary's Academy Opened. — Schools Re-
opened at Oregon City and St. Paul. — Other Early
Schools. — The Pioneer Sisters of Providence

1. Father Croke, First Pastor of Portland.

With the decline of Oregon City, the town of Portland grew rapidly in importance. The first movement
towards the erection of a Catholic church in Portland
was begun in the fall of 1851, when Rev. James Croke
was authorized by the Archbishop to solicit funds for
that purpose. About $600 was secured through sub-
scriptions of residents of Portland and half a block of
ground was purchased from Captain J. H. Couch in
the vicinity of Fifth and Couch Streets. There the building was commenced. While the church was being
erected the Catholics of Portland assisted at Mass in
a private residence until the completion of the little
sacristy at the end of the church, where Mass was celebrated for the first time at midnight, Christmas eve,
1851. Two months later the work was sufficiently ad-

vanced to have the building dedicated. Rough benches answered the purpose of pews and the whole interior of the edifice was unfinished when on February 22, 1852, the ceremony of dedication was performed by the Archbishop, assisted by Very Rev. J. B. Brouillet, Vicar General of Nesqually, and the pastor, Father Croke. The church remained on its original site until 1854, when the congregation began to realize that the building was too far remote from the people. The road to it was a mere trail through the woods, blocked up by fallen trees, over which those going to church had to make their way. A meeting was called and four lots secured from Benjamin Stark at Third and Stark Streets and the building removed to that location.

2. The Church Moved to New Location.

The following letter from Father Croke gives an account of the moving of the church:

"Portland, March 7, '54.
"My Lord Archbishop:
"I avail myself of the kindness of the Right Reverend Bishop of Nesqually to inform your Lordship by a short letter of how we have progressed with the moving of our church.

"We completed the work, thank God, without the slightest accident and our church now stands on its new site as perfect and as strong as if it were built there. The $500, the amount paid for moving it, has been paid; but we still owe the contractor for the enlargement of the sacristy, which cost about $80. This we expect to pay in a few days. Captains Couch and Flanders have given of their own free will two lots out of the four on which the church formerly stood, and have offered us the remaining two for two hundred dollars. They have thus compromised the matter, and are prepared to make out a full deed for those two lots as soon as we give up the deed which is still in your Lordship's possession — and of which you furnished me a copy. This deed they desired me to write for, as they cannot sell the other two lots until they get this deed. Hence, My Lord, it would be well that you would send it by his Lordship of Nesqually on his return from Willamette. If at Oregon City you can tell him where to find it.

"On last Sunday we had Vespers at 6 o'clock in the afternoon followed by the Benediction of the Most Holy Sacrament and sermon. The church was nearly full.

"Recommending myself to your Lordship's prayers and holy sacrifices, I have the honor to remain

"Your Lordship's very humble and obedient servant,

"JAMES CROKE."

When in 1862 the Archbishop removed his residence from Oregon City to Portland this humble church became his pro-Cathedral.

3. Catholic Census in 1855.

Another letter of Father Croke gives us interesting information about the extent of his missionary operations:

"Portland, May 17, 1855.

"My Lord Archbishop:

"I have the honor to submit to your Lordship a full and complete census not only of the Catholics of Portland and vicinity, but also of all the Missions and stations visited by me in the years 1853-4. I hope you will find it satisfactory. I intended appending to the census of the south a description of the various towns, their relative distances and a general 'itineraire' for the use of a traveling priest, but I have got no time just now but shall take the earliest opportunity of doing so and of also making a kind of ecclesiastical map of the country, showing the different points where Catholics are settled, the most convenient sites for missions, etc.

"You will find at the end of the census a general resumé showing at one glance the Catholic population adult and minor of each town in Oregon, commencing at Jacksonville, which I have taken as the center. Starting from Jacksonville I go south to the southern extremity of your Lordship's jurisdiction, then traveling up the seashore to the Umpqua Valley, commencing again at Canyonville, the extreme southern point of the Umpqua, I travel north to the Willamette, taking in all the various stations to the Calapooia Mountains, thence into the Willamette Valley, traveling north until I join the missionary posts where there are resident clergymen. As I lost some of my notes, and as it is impossible for a priest in a flying mission to find out all the Catholics you cannot suppose that I have given the names of all. I have only given the names of those I have actually seen with one or two exceptions. You will find by the report that the entire number of Catholics in the Rogue River, Umpqua and Willamette Valleys amounts to:

"Adults 239
Minors under 12 64
                                                    ——
Total 303

"Of these you have in the Rogue River:
Adults 100
Minors . . . . 5—105
Umpqua Valley:
Adults 65
Minors . . . . 20— 85
Willamette Valley:
Adults 74
Minors . . . . 39—113
                                                    ——303

"I have the honor to remain Your Lordship's humble and obedient servant,

"JAS. CROKE, Mis."

4. The Archbishop Secures the Sisters of the Holy Names.

When Archbishop Blanchet returned from South America in 1857, he learned that his brother, the Bishop of Nisqually, had induced the Sisters of Charity of Providence in Montreal to accept a foundation at Vancouver. Further, Bishop Demers had applied to the Sisters of St. Anne to establish a Convent at Victoria. The Archbishop determined to seek aid in securing religious for his diocese from Bishop Bourget, at whose hands he had received episcopal consecration. He at once secured a block at what is now Fifth and Market Streets, Portland, on which stood an untenanted frame building. With this location and accommodation to offer he set out for Montreal to find Sisters to open a school. Acting under the advice of their founder, Bishop Bourget, the Sisters of the Holy Names of Jesus and Mary responded to the call of the Archbishop. Twelve devoted Sisters, with Mother Alphonse as Superior, left Montreal in September and after a long and at times perilous sea voyage, reached Portland on October 21, 1859. These Sisters opened St. Mary's Academy in humble quarters on the site of the present location of the Academy and College and again lighted the torch of Christian education in the archdiocese.

5. St. Mary's Academy Opened.

The author of *Gleanings of Fifty Years* writes of the arrival of the Sisters: "Even St. Francis of Assisi would have had no reason to complain of the homage paid to 'Lady Poverty' in the first humble domicile of the Sisters of the Holy Names in Portland. The luxury of bedsteads and mattresses was reserved for more prosperous days; the carpet-bags of the travelers were their pillows; the lately purchased blankets by some unexpected process of multiplication, sufficed for the covering of the twelve Sisters. Was theirs a peaceful slumber on their bed of boards, or was it haunted by tearful visions of old home comforts? The answer is told by the joyful note of courage ringing through the convent annals." (Page 73.) The new school was opened November 6, 1859, with six pupils. Ten days later a little orphan girl was received as the first boarder. For some years a large percentage of the smaller girl boarders were orphans. Towards the end of November a class was opened for boys.

6. Schools Reopened at Oregon City and St. Paul.

On April 23, 1860, the Sisters established a school at Oregon City, where the Archbishop still resided. The blight that rested on Oregon City was not removed until the State returned McLoughlin's Land Claim to his heirs in October, 1862. Two months before the Legislative Assembly took this action, Archbishop Blanchet removed to Portland and the convent school was not re-opened in the fall of that year. On February 1, 1861, the Sisters opened a school at St. Paul in the building vacated by the Sisters of Notre Dame. A new class of settlers had taken up farms around St. Paul after the decimation of the population by the rush to the gold mines, and French Prairie again wore an air of prosperity. Here Father Fabian Malo was pastor to a devoted flock. The very winter following the re-establishment of the school at St. Paul there came a terrific flood that swept away the village of Champoeg, causing great loss of life. The flood was followed by intense cold that blocked the Willamette River with ice. Lack of fuel and provisions produced great suffering that necessitated bringing two of the exhausted Sisters and all the remaining pupils from St. Paul to St. Mary's Academy in Portland.

7. Other Early Schools.

In August, 1861, under the direction of Father Patrick Mackin, Pastor of Portland, the Sisters opened a school for boys beside the church on Third and Stark Streets, and on the reconstruction of the Academy in 1862 a home was provided for orphan boys. The Sisters of the Holy Names extended their school work to Salem in 1863. Here the few Catholic families in what was then a strong Methodist community were under the spiritual care of Rev. Leopold Dielman. An unused Masonic hall was purchased and converted into a convent. In the autumn of 1864 at the invitation of Rev. L. Vermeesch, the Sisters established a school at The Dalles, and the following year became pioneers of Catholic education in Southern Oregon by opening a school at Jacksonville at the request of the pastor, Rev. F. X. Blanchet. It was here that Father Croke had built a church in 1858. It was here too that the Sisters had soon an opportunity of devoting themselves to works of charity as well as of education. In 1869 an epidemic of smallpox broke out and for two months the Sisters

administered to the suffering and dying regardless of
their own health. The heroism endeared them to every
class of the little community.

8. The Pioneer Sisters of Providence.

Bishop Blanchet of Nesqually applied to Bishop
Bourget of Montreal in 1856 for Sisters of Providence.
On November 3 of that year five Sisters of Providence
left Montreal by direction of Bishop Bourget for the
Western Mission. They sailed on the steamship Illinois
for Panama. Crossing the Isthmus they embarked for
San Francisco and thence to Astoria, where they arrived December 8, 1856. On the same day they proceeded on the Brother Jonathan and reached their
destination at Vancouver, Washington Territory. The
first Superior was Mother Joseph, a heroic woman
whose name will always be associated with deeds of
mercy and charity in the pioneer history of the Pacific
Northwest. For two months the new arrivals suffered
many privations before their house was fitted up for
use. In February, 1857, they opened a little school
with seven pupils, which rapidly grew in numbers.
The same year two orphans were received by them.
The following year, April 9, 1858, St. Joseph's Hospital was opened in Vancouver.

The Sisters of Providence opened a school at Walla
Walla at the invitation of the pastor, Father Brouillet,
February 18, 1864. On November 25, the previous

year, they established a school at Steilacoom. This school was closed in 1875 when the population migrated to the new town of Tacoma. St. Vincent's Hospital, Portland, was opened May 10, 1875; Providence Hospital, Seattle, at the invitation of pioneer Father Prefontaine, May 2, 1877; the Hospital at Walla Walla, February 27, 1880; Sacred Heart Hospital, Spokane, April 30, 1886; St. Mary's Hospital, New Westminster, B. C., July 6, 1886.

CHAPTER EIGHTEEN

MISSIONARY WORK IN SOUTHERN OREGON

1. Father Croke Visits Salem and Albany.

Father James Croke, who built the first Church in Portland, was also the first Catholic missionary to visit the southwestern section of Oregon. His letters to Archbishop Blanchet, from which the following extracts are taken, are full of interest.

"Jesse Applegate's, Umpqua Valley,
"August 9, 1853.

"My Lord:

"I arrived here this evening after a ride of 32 miles today. I stopped with Mr. Dubois at Salem, and was very hospitably received by him. I saw no house that would answer as a church for the moment, but there is a large room over the store of Wm. Griswold, which could be rented cheap whenever required, $5.00 for a Sunday. I met no Catholic at Salem but Mr. Dubois. O'Reilly is at Rogue River and Mr. Sheely, the lawyer, was at Scottsburgh. I passed through Santiam City and Syracuse and got to Albany the day I left Salem (Thursday). Albany is a considerable town about 24 miles south of Salem. It is built on a large plain eight miles from Marysville, and is supported by a very extensive country. Judging from the appearance of the town it is likely to progress rapidly and become a post of some importance. I called upon the proprietors, Messrs. Monteith, two brothers, to endeavor to get some lots. They appear to be very liberally disposed, but refused to give a deed for lots until we were going to build. They offered two lots in the very center of the town, but only on condition that we would commence to erect a church at furthest next Spring. Of course, I could not accept them on those conditions. I found old O'Reilly on his claim fourteen miles south of Marysville. As my horse was tired, and as it was approaching Sunday, I thought it better to remain with him in order to have an opportunity of saying Mass on Sunday. His house is a most miserable hovel and so small that I'd scarcely find a corner to fix me up an altar. I succeeded, however, in arranging a few boards against the wall, and having spread upon them my altar-cloths and ornaments celebrated the first Mass that was ever said in this part of the country. All the neighborhood are very bigoted against the Catholics, and hold O'Reilly in abhorrence. He received the Sacraments of Confession and Communion, and appears to me to be a very good old man. His wife and children are Protestants, but very well disposed towards the Catholic religion. His wife, in fact, believes in it, and is reading Catholic books. I promised to spend some days there when returning in order to instruct her, and receive her into the Church if properly disposed."

2. Difficulties of Missionary Life.

"Kouse Bay, Lower Umpqua,
"August 26, 1853.

"Monseigneur:

"Since last I have had the honor of writing to Your Lordship, many circumstances have occurred to retard my progress. I am already heartily tired of my missionary tour, and anxiously look forward to the day when I shall be able to return to civilized life and to the society of virtuous friends. Through all this country, with very few exceptions, the state of morality is at its lowest ebb, the few Catholics even that I meet are so only in name, and I assure Your Lordship that the prospects for a missionary are discouraging and gloomy in the extreme; and to add to his mortifications the priest is not only obliged to breathe an atmosphere of corruption, but he is deprived of the happiness of celebrating the divine sacrifice of the Mass, frequently even on Sundays. The only consolation that he has is to pray that God will have mercy on his people, and to unite his intention with those who have the happiness of assisting at the holy offices of the Church. It is only when deprived of that sacred privilege that we can properly appreciate the consolation of our holy religion and the comforts of offering up the divine sacrifice of the Mass."

3. Jacksonville Smaller Than Portland.

"Jacksonville, September 20, 1853.

"My Lord Archbishop:

"I have now visited all the towns in Southern Oregon, and, I think, have acquired a pretty correct idea of the religious prospects of the country. Though not so bright and cheering as a missionary may desire, still they are not altogether hopeless, and I am sure, that in the course of time with patience and persevering exertion aided by a reasonable amount of money, some good may be effected in this part of the country. A permanent missionary post with at least two priests should be established in some central position from which all the countries could be conveniently and regularly visited. A flying mission is useless, or at least the good resulting from it is but partial and by no means abiding. The Catholics here are so few and in general so lukewarm that it requires some time for a priest to hunt them out, and even then it is not in one day that he can inspire them with the proper dispositions. A priest, in order to do good amongst them, must become personally acquainted with them, must follow their motions from place to place, particularly here at the mines where the population is so uncertain and so floating. He must have an accurate idea of the country, must visit his post regularly, and, above all, must be supplied with the funds necessary to defray his expenses — and then, with the grace of God, some good may be reasonably expected to result from his missionary labors.

"I intend preaching here next Sunday in the court house. Jacksonville is a considerable town, but a good deal smaller than Portland. The population consists principally of miners, packers, storekeepers and gamblers, and there are very few families. Tivault and Angel, formerly of Oregon City, live near Jacksonville. As I have already visited Scottsburgh and the Coast, the following is the plan I propose adopting in my journey home. From here to Canyon, where there are a few Canadians with whom I intend spending a few days. There are some dozen capitalists near Winchester. I shall stay one Sunday there to give them an opportunity of assisting at Mass and attending to the religious duties. From thence to Salem through Marysville, where I intend spending another Sunday. When my business is done in Salem I cross the Willamette and visit the upper Yamhill settlement as far as Dayton and Lafayette and perhaps the Guchtins Plains. I cross the Willamette again at Champoeg and hope to spend a few days with Father Mengarini to revive myself a little before starting for Oregon City."

"Salem, Wednesday, October 26, 1853.
"My Lord Archbishop:
"I arrived in Salem this forenoon from the Santiam country about 11 o'clock. Since then I have been about town a good deal looking for a house to let. There are few vacant in any convenient position and those would only be rented by the month. You would have to pay as much for one Sunday in the month, as if you had it in use for every day. On those conditions I did not wish to rent one until I have further instructions from you. The most convenient place in town is a large room which formerly belonged to the Freemasons, but which is now vacant. It can be rented either by the day or by the month. As the owner of it is not now in Salem, I have not been able to know the terms, but I am sure it will be moderate.

"As I informed your Lordship in my letter from Jacksonville, I left that town about the end of September. Having come through The Canyon on the third day from Jacksonville I left the main road and followed up the South Fork of the Umpqua towards its source. I met some Canadian and halfbreed families living on it. I passed one Sunday in the neighborhood, and then came on to Winchester, where I mustered a small congregation on the following Sunday. I successively visited all the towns and valleys where I thought I could find a Catholic, and here I am at present just arrived at Salem. As I have done all my business here today, I don't intend waiting here for Sunday as the season is too far advanced to waste three days. I expected to have been here for last Sunday, but I was detained longer than I anticipated after I crossed the Calapooia Mountains. I spent some days at old O'Reilly's, instructed his wife and baptized her on last Sunday morning before Mass. On tomorrow I leave here for Cincinnati, thence I go to Dayton and cross the river at Baptistes Dagnine for the purpose of changing horses at the missions as my Indian pony is almost worn out.

"Your very humble and obedient servant,

"J. CROKE."

4. Plans for a Church at Jacksonville.

Father Croke's health gave way under the severe trial to which his extensive mission subjected him. In 1857 he went to California and became affiliated with the archdiocese of San Francisco. When Archbishop Blanchet returned from South America, he wrote to Father Croke inviting him to return to his old mission and build a church at Jacksonville. The following letters tell the result:

"Jacksonville, November 9, 1858.

"My Lord Archbishop:

"I have the honor to acknowledge the receipt of Your Grace's two letters, one from Canonville, and the other, on last evening, from Roseburg. I was sorry to learn by your letter from Canonville of your sufferings and adventures during the first few days after leaving here, but I feel grateful that no serious accident occurred. Buggy riding in this country is rather adventurous, as I know by my own experience. As I leave Jacksonville today for Yreka in order to continue my mission I write Your Grace a very brief account of my proceedings and success thus far.

"On the Sunday after your departure from here I said Mass in Jacksonville, and on the following morning started for Althouse, via Sterlingville and Applegate, in order to collect. I am sure your Lordship will feel glad to learn that the Lord blessed the work and that I succeeded admirably well. I arrived at Sailor Diggings, seventy miles from Jacksonville, on Tuesday evening at 8 o'clock, and early on the following morning commenced collecting in a place called Allen Gulch, where the greater part of the miners are working. In two days I collected there $400 in cash, a sum far above my most sanguine expectations for a place where there are not more than seventy men in all, and where they have been several months idle for want of water. Every man on the Gulch — Catholic, Protestant and Orangeman, gave something. The Catholics, God bless them, gave nobly. In the friend's house where I generally stop, I raised $200 in cash, $100 from himself, $50 from his partner and $50 from his hands. This young

man's name is Frank Larkins, and this is not the first
time that I have had reason to be grateful for his generosity. I gave no credit, took no names down until I
received the money, and thus I realized the $400 in cash.

5. At the Forks of Althouse Creek.

"From Allen Gulch I started on Thursday for
Althouse Creek, a distance of ten miles. As the mountains along the creek are very rough, and the miners
generally work in the most rugged ravines and in the
bed of the creek, I was obliged to leave my horse at the
'town' called Browntown and take it on foot for three
days, traveling on an average twenty-five miles a day.
At 8 o'clock on Friday I started up the creek with a
Catholic young man as guide and at 5 o'clock that
evening had $200 more collected in cash. The miners
are so scattered and the road so rough that I only made
four miles in a direct line driving the whole day, though
I suppose I walked at least twenty-five. I stopped that
night at a little trading post called "Grass Flat" and
on the following morning continued my journey with
another young man as guide for the forks of Althouse
Creek. I made $198 that day. Making in all for
Althouse, with a few other dollars which I received,
over $400. There are a great deal more miners here
than in Allen Gulch, but very many of them are just
returned from Fraser River, and are scarcely making
their board. They all, however, paid a little. I took
so small as fifty cents in a grocery store from a man
who was going to spend it for whiskey. I told him it
would buy two pounds of nails. The next day being
Sunday, I had no vestments (expecting to have been

back in Jacksonville) and could not say Mass. I am less scrupulous than your Grace on the point of traveling on Sunday, so I walked back by a better road along the side of mountains my two days' journey in three hours to Browntown. That evening at three o'clock I started for Kerbyville; called to see Mr. Allen, who lives near it, for his subscription, but received nothing from him. The next evening I started for Jacksonville and collected $50 more on the road and arrived in Jacksonville on Tuesday night, having been absent eight days. I was very sorry not to be able to say Mass on All Saints and All Souls, but it was impossible for me to get back sooner without leaving my job unfinished.

6. Construction Begun.

"Thus you see, My Lord, that in the neglected part of Oregon I collected in a few days in cash the sum of $856 for a church to be built sixty-five miles from them. This was very fortunate for otherwise I could scarcely meet the expenses as I have been able to collect only $30 in Jacksonville since you left. They all promise, will give their names very readily to be paid at some future day, but names won't build a church and I can't spend much time idly. They promise, however, to pay when I come back. The poor miners, on whom alone I count, have nothing just now. My plan is to go to Yreka, and to return when the rain sets in and spend one or two days collecting before my final departure for Salmon River. Your Lordship is no doubt anxious to hear about the church. It was raised on the Octave of All Saints, November 8, but as the carpenters are busy finishing Anderson's house (which will be finished in a few days) they are not able to go ahead as yet very rapidly. They have two carpenters at work dressing the siding. I have had a good solid wall of rock pointed with mortar built all around under the sills. It is nearly two feet square at the corners. It cost about $50. Your Lordship's suggestion about the height of the piers arrived too late to be attended to. The church, however, looks very high and when completed will be a neat building. It looks very short. It is 36 by 23."

7. Recalled to San Francisco.

"Jacksonville, O. T., December 15, '58. "My Lord Archbishop:

"I received your Grace's favor of November addressed to me at Yreka and was glad to learn that you got home safe. I left Yreka for this place on Monday, December 13th, and leave tomorrow morning for home. I regret that I could not spend more than two days here. I have yet a good deal to do in Yreka, and have received a letter from Archbishop Alemany desiring me to be in San Francisco immediately after Christmas.

"On coming here from Yreka, I was surprised to find so little done to the church in my absence. The carpenters give for excuse that they had not the necessary lumber for the window frames, which must be thoroughly seasoned. They have planed all the siding and flooring, have all the lumber required now and will go ahead as quick as necessary with the work. I am sure your Grace sees the necessity of sending a priest to the district as soon as possible. If possible he should speak English perfectly and preach well. All here send your Grace their respectful compliments. If at any time, consistently with obedience to my Superior, I can do any good for any portion of Oregon, I will be happy in being at your Lordship's disposal. I hope to have the pleasure of seeing you soon in San Francisco, and recommending myself to your Lordship's prayers I have the honor to remain, with due esteem and respect,

"Your very humble and obedient servant,

"JAMES CROKE."

Father Croke now bade adieu to Oregon. He afterwards became Vicar General of San Francisco. He is remembered as one of the ablest and most devoted priests of pioneer days in the West. He was a brother of Archbishop Croke of Cashel.

CHAPTER NINETEEN

AMONG THE INDIANS

Obstacles to Successful Work Among the Indians. —
Missionary Rivalry. — The Work of Father Mesplie.
— Appointed United States Post Chaplain. — Father
Croquet at Grand Ronde. — President Grant's Indian
Policy.—Commissioners Unfriendly to Catholic Cause.
— Catholic Indian Mission Bureau Established

1. Obstacles to Successful Work Among the Indians.

The story of the beginning of Catholic Indian missions among the Indians of Oregon has been told in an earlier chapter. For an understanding of the work among them subsequent to the establishment of the hierarchy (1846) we must bear in mind the following facts. The Indians of Western Oregon were much inferior both physically and morally to their brethren in the Rocky Mountains. This condition became accentuated when the whites came into the country, for the Indians of the interior met the whites only occasionally while those of the coast had an opportunity to learn all the worst vices of the whites from daily intercourse. Even the mission schools do not seem to have helped the Willamette Valley savages. Medorem Crawford was a teacher at the Methodist Mission school at Salem in the forties. He writes of the work in which he was engaged as follows: "The general result of all that work on the part of the missionaries here was deleterious to the Indians. As fast as we learnt the boys to talk English they would learn to swear. I could hardly find an exception but that they turned out the worst Indians in the country." (Ms. A. 19, page 5, Bancroft Lib.) A second fact to be borne in mind is that during the administration of Dr. McLoughlin, that is until 1846, the savages were at peace and the work of the Catholic missionaries went on apace. But after the Whitman massacre and the Cayuse war, the relations of the whites and Indian tribes were scarcely ever satisfactory and missionary work necessarily greatly impeded. Thus Father Brouillet established a mission at St. Ann's, among the Cayuses, on November 27, 1847. With the aid of an interpreter he translated the prayers into their language but hardly had he begun his work when hostilities broke out with the whites and interrupted the mission.

2. Missionary Rivalry.

Another obstacle to effective evangelization of the Indians was the bitter rivalry between the various missionary bands. When Bishop Blanchet met Dr. Whitman at Fort Walla Walla in 1847, the latter remarked with some heat: "I know very well for what purpose you have come." "All is known," replied the Bishop, "I come to labor for the conversion of the Indians, and even of the Americans if they are willing to listen to me." At an earlier date when the Indian chiefs were being taught to explain the Archbishop's "Catholic Ladder" to their people, Mrs. Spalding (wife of the minister at Lapwai) employed her artistic talents in painting a Protestant ladder, which aimed to show the broad road of the Catholic Church as the way to perdition and the straight and narrow path of Protestantism as the way to heaven. (This "Protestant Ladder" is in the library of Mr. Frederick V. Holman, at Portland.)

3. The Work of Father Mesplie.

In view of these facts it is not surprising that the later missions among the Indians did not achieve the success which the earlier attempts promised. Nevertheless there was no lack of zeal on the part of the missionaries. The mantle of DeSmet seems to have fallen on Father Toussaint Mesplie. Ordained to the priesthood in 1850, he had already begun his work among the savages in the Willamette Valley. In 1849 he opened a mission among the Chinooks at the mouth of the Columbia and attended the various tribes in the neighborhood. Here too he visited the Catholic soldiers at Fort Astoria and laid the foundation for his extended and valuable service as army chaplain. After his ordination he was sent to The Dalles, where he took charge of St. Peter's Mission and attended to the spiritual wants of the Wascoes and various confederated tribes who were later placed in the Warm Springs Reservation. He gained such influence among these tribes that in the fall of 1855 when the Indian outbreak began, he prevailed upon the Wasco tribe not to join with the others against the whites. During the period of hostilities he was in communication with the various military posts and kept them informed of the hostile plans of the savages.

4. Appointed United States Post Chaplain.

In 1863 Father Mesplie was sent to take charge of the new mining settlements that were springing up in Idaho Territory. While attending to the spiritual wants of the Irish miners, he did not forget the needs of the various Indian tribes in the neighborhood. He found time also to perform the duties of chaplain to the soldiers at Fort Boise. In 1864 the Shoshone and Bannock tribes of Indians became very troublesome. These Indians held full control of the emigrant and stage roads leading to Oregon and Washington Territory. Every few days, says an eyewitness,[1] the mangled corpse of some stage driver, frontier settler or venturesome miner or unfortunate emigrant would be brought to Fort Boise for interment, a victim to the brutality of the savages.

---

1. John A. O'Farrell, who donated the block of land for the first Catholic Church in Boise.

Father Mesplie set out for the camps of the hostile tribes and showed them the error of their ways with such effect that he gathered more than two hundred of them on the parade ground of Fort Boise and baptized them all on a single day. It is reliably asserted that none of these Indians who were converted by Father Mesplie ever again bore arms against the whites. In recognition of his services he was appointed United States Post Chaplain in August, 1872, and assigned to Fort Boise.

5. Father Croquet at Grand Ronde.

Another name inseparably connected with the later Indian missions in Oregon is that of Father Adrian Croquet, a native of Belgium, who arrived at Oregon City in 1859 to devote himself to the spiritual welfare of the savages. Father Croquet was initiated into his new field of labor by Father Mesplie, whom he accompanied "on an apostolic expedition among several Indian tribes dwelling along the banks of the Columbia River in the neighborhood of Mount Hood. We were everywhere most affectionately received, the chiefs honoring us by offering the calumet." In October, 1860, Father Croquet was definitely settled in the Grand Ronde Indian Reservation in Yamhill County. In reference to his first visit to the Reservation he writes: "We were most cordially welcomed by the Captain and the officers of Fort Yamhill, which borders on the Reservation. We celebrated Mass at the Fort, preached

REV. ADRIAN CROQUET

and admitted to the Sacraments the soldiers and the members of a few Catholic families occupying land in the neighborhood. The Indians were not forgotten; the Agent, Mr. Miller, giving us full scope to do all the good we could. He is a most estimable official, who takes the poor Redman's interests to heart, and whose sympathies are all with the Catholic missionaries." Father Croquet also had charge of the Siletz Reservation but there he was not able to report the same kind treatment on the part of the Agent that he had experienced at Grand Ronde. He was successful, however, in gaining the good will of the Indians. After nearly forty years of untiring and devoted service of the spiritual welfare of his Indian brethren the saintly old missionary returned (1898) to his fatherland to spend his last days. Father Croquet was the uncle of Cardinal Mercier.

6. President Grant's Indian Policy.

The constant outbreaks on the part of the savages resulted in the quartering of military forces among them and the assigning of military agents to take charge of the various Indian stations. In 1870 President Grant inaugurated a new system for the government of the Indians. On December 5 of that year he announced to Congress that he had determined to give all the Indian agencies to "such religious denominations as had heretofore established missions among the Indians." In carrying out this policy many of the Catholic Indian tribes were placed under non-Catholic control. Against this condition, Archbishop Blanchet, under date of July 8, 1871, addressed a strong letter of vigorous and indignant protest to the Commissioner of Indian Affairs. The Archbishop in his letter calls attention to the injustice of this procedure by recounting the work which the Catholic missionaries had done among the savages of the Oregon country from the earliest days. He recalled the work of himself and of Father Demers from Fort Colville to Chinook Point and from Eastern Oregon to the Fraser River; of Father DeSmet and his zealous co-workers among the Flatheads and other Indian tribes of the Rocky Mountains; the establishment of the Yakima mission by Father D'Herbomez, O. M. I., subsequently Bishop of British Columbia, with his indefatigable brethren of the Oblates in the year 1847 and its maintenance until the Indian war of 1855 forced him to retire; the mission of Father Brouillet among the Cayuse tribe in 1847, and after the war, the continuance of that mission at Walla Walla by Father Chirouse, O. M. I., from 1852 to 1856, when another outbreak forced him to abandon it, and its further maintenance at Umatilla Reservation by Father Vermeesch from 1866 to 1871. The Archbishop also instanced the mission of Father Mesplie at The Dalles and his teaching among the Wasco and allied tribes until these Indians were transferred to the Warm Springs Reservation and finally the mission at Grand Ronde from 1860 to 1871 established by Father Croquet, who built a church and opened a school among the Indians there. The Yakima Indians, among whom Fathers Chirouse and D'Herbomez had labored for many years, were in 1870 placed under Protestant control.

7. Commissioners Unfriendly to Catholic Cause.

In view of all these facts the Archbishop protested that a grave injustice was being done to the Catholic Church. Acting as spokesman for all the Bishops of the country in the interest of the Indian missions he carried on a voluminous correspondence with Mr. Delano, Secretary of the Interior, and had the Archbishops and Bishops protest to the same authority. Few results could reasonably be hoped for. Father DeSmet, who was in close touch with the administration through his employment as a peace emissary among the savages, wrote to the Archbishop from St. Louis under date of March 11, 1871, that the Administration of the Commission on Indian Affairs was exclusively Protestant and disinclined to assign any Catholic agents to our Indian missions. He had been invited in January of that year to Washington to assist at a meeting of the Indian Commissioners appointed by President Grant. He found himself the only Catholic in a large gathering called to apportion the Indian stations to the various denominations. The apportionment was made, he adds, with but little exception, to the advantage of the Protestant sects. This was of course a high-handed policy. The Indians were not consulted about the religion that was to be thrust upon them. Thus thousands of Catholic Indians who were most anxious for Catholic missionaries to minister to them and to instruct their children, were denied the elementary right of choosing their own religion. In the case of the Yakima and Nez Perces Reservations, the Indian Commissioners in June, 1871, permitted the Catholics to build chapels but the station was under Protestant control. Agent Wilbur at the Yakima Reservation refused the Catholic priests entrance to the reservation to teach and to administer sacraments to the sick. The agent frequently denied to parents the privilege of taking their children to the Catholic Church for Mass and instruction.

8. Catholic Indian Mission Bureau Established.

The situation developed a very acrimonious controversy between the Protestant and Catholic missionaries and sympathizers. The controversy waxed to a white heat when Rev. H. H. Spalding revived the dying embers of the Whitman discussion and invented the Whitman myth to destroy the credit of the Catholic Indian missionaries. Spalding's vile pamphlet was published in 1871 as a Senate Executive Document at the instance of Secretary Delano. This document became the official statement of the Whitman Legend which has been discussed in a former chapter. In the course of this protracted conflict it became evident to the Archbishop and the Bishop of Nesqually that the large interests at stake required the continual presence of an authorized representative of the Catholic Indian Missions at Washington. For this purpose Father Brouillet, who was thoroughly acquainted with the missionary field, was chosen and appointed Director of the Catholic Indian Mission Bureau in 1874. This bureau was reorganized in 1879 and continues to represent efficiently the cause of the Catholic Indians.

NOTE. Benjamin Alvord, who was stationed at The Dalles in 1853, as Captain of the Fourth Infantry, wrote in 1873 of the services of Fathers Mesplie and Pandosy, O. M. I.: "Father Mesplie was a Catholic priest having charge of a mission (not a mile from the military post of Fort Dalles) to the Wascoes, who were friendly and have always remained so, fighting on our side down to the recent Modoc war.

"But the hostile Indians were Yakimas, Palouse and Cayuse, and one of their principal centers, one hundred miles north-northeast from The Dalles, was near what is now Fort Simcoe, where there was another mission under Father Pandosy. Early in the spring of 1853, Father Mesplie showed me confidentially a letter to him from Father Pandosy, making known a gigantic combination of all the tribes on the frontier. I took immediate steps to report to the Government these schemes of the Indians." Had the warning been heeded the Indian war of 1855 might have been avoided.

OLD CATHEDRAL AND REV. J. F. FIERENS

CHAPTER TWENTY

LAST YEARS OF ARCHBISHOP BLANCHET

Father Fierens Becomes Pastor of Portland. — Erection of the Vicariate of Idaho. — Golden Jubilee of Archbishop Blanchet. — Departs for the Vatican Council. — "Catholic Sentinel" Established in 1870. — St. Michael's College Opened. — St. Vincent's Hospital Established in Portland. — Active Administration of Archbishop Blanchet Closes. — Archbishop Seghers Becomes Coadjutor.—Archbishop Blanchet's Farewell Pastoral. — Death of Archbishop Blanchet

I. Father Fierens Becomes Pastor of Portland.

The Archbishop had taken up his residence in Portland in August, 1862. The following year Father J. F. Fierens, who had been Pastor of Jacksonville, was appointed to the pro-Cathedral, a charge which he held continuously for thirty years, until his death in 1893. In 1878, under the direction of Father Fierens, the old church structure was taken down and on the Feast of the Assumption of the same year the cornerstone of a Gothic Cathedral was laid. For a quarter of a century the zealous and energetic pastor was one of the foremost men in public view in Portland.

2. Erection of the Vicariate of Idaho.

In 1868, Archbishop Blanchet was relieved of the care of the eastern portion of his diocese by the erection

on March 3rd of that year of the Vicariate Apostolic
of Idaho. The Second Plenary Council of Baltimore
had requested this step of the Holy See. Father Lootens,
who had gone with Bishop Demers to Vancouver in
1852 as a pioneer missionary, was consecrated in August of that year as Bishop of Castaballa and Vicar
Apostolic of Idaho. When Bishop Lootens went to
Idaho Territory early in 1869 he found there only two
priests, Fathers Mesplie and Poulin. The mines which
had been opened had not prospered; the rich mines of
Idaho were still to be prospected. Meanwhile the
miners left the territory in large numbers and the Catholic population was notably diminished. The Sisters
of the Holy Names who had established a school at
Idaho City in 1868 were forced to close their doors
within two years. Two of the best churches were destroyed by fire and the small missions of the Vicariate
were badly encumbered by debt. In 1876 Bishop Lootens, broken in health, resigned his position and retired
to Victoria. The Vicariate of Idaho remained under
the jurisdiction of the Archbishop of Oregon City until
the consecration of Bishop Glorieux as titular Bishop
of Apollonia in 1885. The Diocese of Boise was
erected August 25, 1893.

3. Golden Jubilee of Archbishop Blanchet.

In 1869 Archbishop Blanchet solemnly celebrated
the fiftieth anniversary of his ordination to the priest-

hood. In a circular to the clergy of the archdiocese announcing the jubilee he writes: "On the 18th of the present month of July — which falls on a Sunday, as in 1819 — if it please God, we will enjoy a great favor, which, considering the uncertainty and fickleness of human life, we hardly expected, in the midst of our long missionary life in hard and incessant labors in this country and elsewhere. This favor is that of receiving from the Most High, the grace of completing a career long enough to be able to celebrate the holy sacrifice of the Mass on the occasion of the jubilee of the fiftieth anniversary of our ordination to the priesthood, and of our first Mass on the following day. So signal a favor fills our soul with gladness and gratitude and moves us also to invite you and all the members of your devoted congregation to join with us in humble and fervent prayer in order to render solemn thanksgiving to Almighty God for so great a favor."

Before the Pontifical Mass celebrated by the Archbishop, assisted by his brother, the Bishop of Nesqually, the Catholic Library and Christian Doctrine Society of Portland presented an address of congratulation through a committee of ten representative laymen of the city. "The event of this day," they observe, "reminds us of the fact that during the present year our Holy Father, Pius the Ninth, has likewise had the good fortune of celebrating the jubilee of the fiftieth anniversary of his ordination to the priesthood. As your

Grace will leave in a short time to attend the approaching General Council, we take this occasion to say that our hearts and our prayers will be with you in your far distant journey. We pray that you may have a safe and pleasant voyage to the Holy See of St. Peter, that the wisdom of heaven may guide and direct all your labors, and that on the completion of the deliberations of the Ecumenical Council you may have a speedy and safe return to your loving and dutiful children in Christ in this Archdiocese and that you may be long spared to live and labor in your chosen field."

4. Departs for the Vatican Council.

Early in October of the same year the Archbishop addressed a pastoral on the Infallibility of the Church to the Catholics of Portland on the eve of his departure for Rome to assist at the Vatican Council. At that Council the Archbishop was a strong advocate of the opportuneness of the declaration of Papal Infallibility and prepared a sermon to be delivered to the assembled Bishops urging the promulgation of the decree. It is interesting to recall that the Archbishop in going to Rome traveled eastward from San Francisco over the newly completed Union Pacific Railway, which was to exert so large an influence in the material progress of the West. In his journal of the trip the Archbishop tells of crossing the ocean with Father Ireland (later Archbishop) of St. Paul.

5. "Catholic Sentinel" Established in 1870.

The first issue of the *Catholic Sentinel* appeared in February, 1870, with H. L. Herman and J. F. Atkinson as publishers. A prospectus tells us that the publishers have decided to undertake the task "in consequence of the kind encouragement and promised support of the Very Rev. J. F. Fierens, Vicar General and Administrator of the Archdiocese." Father Fierens was fully awake to the necessity of an efficient Catholic press to promote the cause of religion and morality. He writes as follows: "We judge the time most desirable and opportune for a Catholic publication in this State, when now in Ecumenical Council the Catholic world is assembled in the Eternal City of Rome; when undoubtedly our Church, by sectarian and infidel newspapers will be assailed, misrepresented and abused, it behooves us more than ever to defend her, and to enlighten and disabuse so many deluded and misguided people." The new paper received the hearty approval of the Bishops of the Province. The Archbishop wrote from Rome under date of March 12, 1870: "The first number was received here on the 10th inst., and it took me indeed by surprise, as it was altogether unexpected, but it was most heartily welcomed. Many warm wishes for its success and long life!" The *Sentinel* remained for years under the able editorship of the pioneer publisher, Mr. S. J. McCormick, one of the first mayors of Portland.

6. St. Michael's College Opened.

In 1871 St. Michael's College for boys was opened at Portland. More than sixty pupils presented themselves the opening day, August 28. The work of building the college was undertaken and brought to completion in three months. The success of the school was largely due to the energetic efforts of Father Fierens and the capable direction of the first principal, Rev. A. J. Glorieux, later Bishop of Boise. Subsequently the school passed into the charge of Rev. Bernard Orth, who later became Archbishop of Victoria. Contemporary accounts tell us that the College had a brass band, telegraph apparatus, physical laboratory and a printing office. The students published a monthly paper, *The Archangel,* which enjoyed a circulation of about 500.

7. St. Vincent's Hospital Established in Portland.

The Sisters of Providence, who had established a hospital in Vancouver in 1858, accepted an invitation to open a similar institution in Portland. The new building was dedicated in the presence of a large assemblage on July 19, 1875. "We may feel proud of our St. Vincent's Hospital," said Father Fierens, in his address at the dedicatory services, "this future home of the sick, as it is the first in the State, and one in which not only Catholics but every citizen is interested, as it admits all religionists. We must also thank the good citizens of Portland who have aided with no sparing hand in its erection; they knew that such enterprises as these are limited in their benefits to no particular creed, but that their good results must affect the entire community. So men who were not of our faith have not hesitated to give of their means to push this enterprise forward."

8. Active Administration of Archbishop Blanchet Closes.

The year 1879 may be considered as the last of the active administration of Archbishop Blanchet. At that time his archdiocese contained twenty-three clergy, twenty-two churches, sixty-eight Sisters, nine academies for girls, one college for boys, four parochial schools for boys, two parochial schools for girls, an orphanage and a hospital. He had secured the care of two Indian reservations, one at Grand Ronde with a Sisters' school, the other at Umatilla with a school directed by the pastor.

9. Archbishop Seghers Becomes Coadjutor.

The last ten years had witnessed a marvelous growth, and the Archbishop feeling that his years were drawing to a close, sought for an assistant on whose shoulders he might lay the burdens of the archdiocese. Such an assistant he found in Bishop Charles John Seghers, who had been consecrated Bishop of Vancouver Island to succeed the pioneer Bishop Demers

Most Rev. C. J. Seghers
Apostle of Alaska
SECOND ARCHBISHOP OF OREGON CITY

in 1873. The extensive territory of Alaska having been attached to the diocese of Vancouver Island Bishop Seghers made a visitation of the mining camps and Indian settlements of that vast region, returning to Victoria in 1878, after fifteen months' absence, winning deservedly the title, "Apostle of Alaska." On his return to Victoria he learned of his appointment as coadjutor to the Archbishop of Oregon. On July 1, 1879, the new Archbishop arrived in Portland, where he was welcomed by the venerable founder of the archdiocese, surrounded by his clergy and laity. "This day of your reception in this Cathedral as my coadjutor and future successor is the happiest day of my life," said Archbishop Blanchet. On behalf of the clergy Father Fierens extended to the new ruler of the archdiocese "united congratulations and our united obedience. Eleven months ago when first your name was mentioned in connection with the coadjutorship of this See, the hearts of both the clergy and the laity were gladdened at the prospect that our venerable and dearly beloved Archbishop Blanchet, who has planted the cross, the standard of Christianity in this diocese, was to be succeeded in the Episcopate by one so capable of carrying on the numerous works of piety, education and charity, which were inaugurated under his watchful and fatherly supervision and we are glad that we can entrust to your solicitude our young institutions and parishes and are confident that you will consolidate the good that has already been done."[1]

10. Archbishop Blanchet's Farewell Pastoral.

After initiating his successor into the work of the archdiocese the venerable Archbishop withdrew wholly from active labors. He published his farewell pastoral on February 27, 1881, announcing the acceptance of his resignation by the Holy Father. The aged prelate approached the altar with tottering steps to address for the last time his beloved congregation. His lips falter but he speaks with the dignity of an apostle: "After sixty-two years of the priesthood; after forty-three years of toilsome labor on this Coast; after an episcopate of thirty-six years; after thirty-five years spent at the head of this Ecclesiastical Province, we may say with the Apostle St. Paul, 'The time of my dissolution is at hand. I have finished my course'; and with Holy Simeon, 'Let therefore the Lord dismiss His servant in peace for truly my eyes have seen the wonderful works of His salvation.' We came to this country accompanied by the late Modeste Demers, the first Bishop of Vancouver Island, in 1838, to preach the true Gospel for the first time; and where then we saw nothing but 'darkness and the shadow of death,' we have now flourishing

---

1. Archbishop Seghers was but one of the many devoted priests who received their preparation for missionary work in the Pacific Northwest at the celebrated University of Louvain in Belgium.

dioceses and vicariates, prosperous missions, a zealous clergy, fervent communities and a Catholic people of whom we expect great works and noble deeds.

"At the age of eighty-six years, we feel that 'we are growing old like a garment' and that our 'generation being at an end' our time has arrived to retire into a place of rest and solitude, in order 'to recount to God all our years in the bitterness of our soul.' Farewell then, beloved and reverend brethren of the priesthood, who have been so often our consolation. Farewell, beloved daughters, Christian virgins, spouses of Jesus Christ, who have so often edified and rejoiced us with the perfume of your virtues. Farewell, beloved children of the laity, who have been so long the object of our concern and of our prayerful solicitude. Farewell, young men, in whom we behold with pleasure the future of the Catholic Church in this country. Farewell, little children, the beloved of Jesus Christ, and the cherished of our hearts. We part now but we have the firm hope of seeing you forever in heaven. Forget not your old and loving spiritual father; forgive him his mistakes and shortcomings; pray for him that his sins may be forgiven and forgotten when he will be called on to give an account of his stewardship." The Archbishop having relinquished entirely the cares of the archdiocese, the Pallium was conferred on his successor on the Feast of the Assumption, 1881.

11. Death of Archbishop Blanchet.

Two years later, June 18, 1883, the Patriarch of the West passed to his reward. Archbishop Seghers at the Pontifical Requiem Mass at the Cathedral pronounced the following words of eulogy with which we may appropriately close our account of the first missionary, first bishop, first metropolitan of the Pacific Northwest; "Do you realize it, beloved brethren? He is the apostle of this coast, the foundation of this mission, the cornerstone of this church; the seed that was sown here and grew into a large, lofty tree was sown by his hand; to him under God we owe the flourishing condition of Christianity in this country; and he is dead! ... Do you know, beloved brethren, that a time will come when the name of Archbishop Blanchet will be coupled with those of Las Casas, the first missionary of Central America, of Marquette and Breboeuf, the pioneers of the cross in Canada and the States of the Atlantic?

"Why? Because he was the first missionary, the apostle of Oregon; he is to Oregon what St. Boniface was to Germany, what St. Augustine was to England, what St. Patrick was to Ireland! And, believe me, our children will envy us the blessing of having seen him, of having conversed with him, of having listened to his voice."

APPENDIX I

LATER YEARS

1. Most Reverend Charles John Seghers, Second Archbishop — 1880-1885.

As noted in the preceding chapter, Bishop Seghers was appointed coadjutor to Archbishop Blanchet in 1878. When the latter withdrew entirely from active duties Seghers became Archbishop (Dec. 20, 1880), and entered energetically on his duties. He traversed a large part of Idaho, Western Montana, eastern and southern Oregon in a tour of visitation, covering 2,300 miles chiefly by stage and on horseback. He had been succeeded in the Diocese of Vancouver Island by Bishop Brondel. While in Rome in 1884 Bishop Seghers secured from Pope Leo XIII the erection of the vicariate of Montana into the Diocese of Helena with Bishop Brondel as first Bishop (March 7, 1884). Difficulty was now experienced in filling the vacant Diocese of Vancouver Island. Much to the admiration of the Holy Father the Archbishop offered to resign his metropolitan see to resume his former work especially with the

MOST REV. WILLIAM H. GROSS

THIRD ARCHBISHOP OF OREGON CITY

Indians of Alaska. Archbishop Seghers returned to Oregon and on March 29, 1885, preached for the last time in the Portland cathedral. A few days later, April 2, he was again Bishop of Vancouver Island. The same year he established two missions in Alaska, one at Sitka, the other at Juneau. On his fifth expedition to Alaska he was brutally murdered (November 28, 1886) by a mentally unbalanced servant named Fuller. The remains of the saintly and scholarly prelate were taken to Victoria for interment.

2. Most Reverend William H. Gross, Third Archbishop — 1885-1898.

The choice of a successor to the See of Oregon City fell upon the Most Rev. William H. Gross, Bishop of Savannah. He arrived in Portland May 23, 1885, accompanied by the Most Rev. A. J. Glorieux, who had been consecrated Bishop of Apollonia *in partibus* and Vicar Apostolic of Idaho in the cathedral at Baltimore by Archbishop Gibbons on April 25. The new Archbishop was born in Baltimore, June 12, 1837. His father was an Alsatian and his maternal grandfather was an Irish exile of 1798. Archbishop Gross was a member of the Redemptorist Order. Ordained in 1864, he served for a time as a military chaplain at Annapolis.

St. Mary's Cathedral, which had been erected on the site of the old frame church at Third and Stark streets in Portland was dedicated by the new Archbishop August 15, 1885. In October of that year he acquired the *Catholic Sentinel* as the property of the Archdiocese. In October, 1887, Cardinal Gibbons visited his old friend at Portland and invested the Archbishop with the pallium in the presence of the Bishops of the Province and a notable gathering of the clergy and laity. In 1889 Archbishop Gross had the satisfaction of seeing opened in his diocese the Benedictine College at Mt. Angel. The Benedictines had founded their community in Oregon in 1882 at the invitation of Archbishop Seghers, temporarily at Gervais, but (1884) permanently at Mt. Angel, so-called for the mother-house at Engelberg, Switzerland. Contemporaneous with the foundation of the Benedictine Fathers in Oregon was the establishment of a community of Benedictine Sisters whose members, eight in number, arrived in Gervais October 30, 1882. In 1888 the Sisters removed from Gervais to Mt. Angel where their mother-house and novitiate now are.

Soon after his arrival in Oregon Archbishop Gross invited the Christian Brothers, who had established flourishing schools in California, to come to Portland to take charge of St. Michael's College which had from its beginning in 1871 been conducted by the diocesan clergy. Early in 1886 the Brothers assumed the direction of the College, which they maintained at its old location at Fifth and Mill streets until the beginning

of the school year in August, 1895, when the College
ceased to exist. The Brothers at this time opened St.
Mary's Parochial School for boys at Fifteenth and Davis
streets. Later they returned to the old location of St.
Michael's College naming their school Blanchet Institute, in honor of the pioneer Archbishop. They remained here until December, 1908, when they occupied the new Christian Brothers' Business College, later
closed.

In 1886 the Archbishop established the Congregation of the Sisters of St. Mary at Sublimity, Oregon.
Five zealous women entered the community on the
Feast of the Assumption of that year. The young community prospered and now conducts a number of flourishing schools in the Archdiocese. One of the earliest
problems to which the Archbishop turned his attention
was the provision of suitable accommodations for the
orphans of the Archdiocese. He secured a farm of
some six hundred acres near Beaverton and had erected
there the necessary buildings, which in 1891, were
placed in the hands of the Sisters of St. Mary, who
undertook the care of the orphan boys and girls. In
the case of the girls they assumed a duty up to this
time performed by the Sisters of the Holy Names. Several years later (1894) the Sisters of St. Mary removed
their motherhouse and novitiate from Sublimity to the
beautiful property near the orphan home. Here, also

in 1893 they established their principal educational institution, St. Mary's Institute for girls and young women.

During these years several religious communities were brought into the Archdiocese. In 1888 the Dominican Sisters came to Portland from California to assume the conduct of St. Joseph's German parochial school. Later they took charge of the parochial school of the Immaculate Heart Parish, Portland, where they conduct Immaculata Academy. In 1892 the Sisters Adorers of the Precious Blood from St. Hyacinthe, Canada, were invited to make a foundation in Oregon and established themselves in their monastery at Mt. Tabor. The Dominican Fathers, in 1894, occupied their convent and church of the Holy Rosary in Portland. At the invitation of Archbishop Gross, the Sisters of Mercy came to Oregon in 1896 and founded the Home for Working Girls (now the Jeanne d'Arc), and later the Home for the Aged, St. Agnes' Baby Home, and three hospitals.

At the suggestion of the Archbishop, the Sisters of the Good Shepherd established a Home of Correction at Park Place, an institution which was later removed to the city of Portland. In 1917 the commodious new St. Rose's Industrial School was built by the Sisters of the Good Shepherd to take the place of their earlier less suitable building.

On April 27, 1898, Archbishop Gross celebrated the twenty-fifth anniversary of his episcopal consecration. There was presented to him on this occasion a residence at Sixteenth and Davis Streets, the gift of his priests and people. Owing to the encroachment of the business district on the old residence portion of the city the use of the cathedral at Third and Stark Streets was discontinued and a modest church building erected at Fifteenth and Davis Streets. The death of the Archbishop occurred at Baltimore, November 14, 1898, after a brief illness.

3. Most Reverend Alexander Christie, Fourth Archbishop — 1899-1925.

Most Rev. Alexander Christie, Bishop of Vancouver Island, was chosen successor to Archbishop Gross and was installed as fourth Archbishop of Oregon City in St. Mary's pro-Cathedral, Portland, on June 15, 1899. He received the pallium from the hands of Archbishop Martinelli, the papal delegate, on May 17, 1900. Born in Vermont in 1848, he came with his parents to Minnesota and there attended St. John's College. His ecclesiastical studies were made at the Grand Seminary, Montreal, where he was ordained to the priesthood for the Archdiocese of St. Paul by Archbishop Fabre, December 22, 1877. On June 29, 1898, he was consecrated Bishop of Vancouver Island.

MOST REV. ALEXANDER CHRISTIE
FOURTH ARCHBISHOP OF OREGON CITY

A few days after his installation Archbishop Christie laid the cornerstone of the new monastery of the Benedictine Fathers at Mt. Angel. The event was to be typical of his work in Oregon, for his time will be known as the building era of the Archdiocese. Contributing to the rapid expansion of the Church in Oregon during this period were the revival of commercial prosperity after the depression of the early nineties and a notable increase in immigration from the eastern states and Europe bearing a larger proportion of Catholics than had been the case in earlier days.

Because of Archbishop Christie's encouragement and direction parishes were multiplied, churches, schools, hospitals, homes for dependent children and old people, were built, the number of diocesan clergy increased, and a large number of religious communities both of men and women were called into the service of the Archdiocese.

The care of the dependent children early claimed his solicitude. Finding the accommodations at Beaverton inadequate for both boys and girls, he transferred the orphan girls to St. Paul, where they were cared for by the Sisters of the Holy Names until 1908, when the Christie Home for Orphan Girls was erected at Marylhurst, on the Willamette above Oswego. Nearby the Sisters of the Holy Names have built their Provincialate and Marylhurst Normal School and, more recently, the splendid group of buildings comprised in Marylhurst College for Women. St. Mary's Home for Orphan Boys in care of the Sisters of St. Mary was augmented in 1924 by a group of new buildings, known as the Levi Anderson Industrial School, made possible by the bequest of Levi Anderson, who left his entire estate to the Archbishop for that purpose.

Shortly after his arrival in Portland the Archbishop acquired the buildings and grounds of the old Portland University, which had been conducted by the Methodists. Re-naming it "Columbia," he opened a school in the autumn of 1901 with a staff of diocesan priests and laymen. The Holy Cross Fathers came in 1902 to take charge of the college, and since then have steadily enlarged its scope. It is now known as the University of Portland.

Among the religious communities which were called into the Archdiocese during the administration of Archbishop Christie were the Jesuits, the Redemptorists, the Franciscans, the Servites, the Paulists, the Capuchins, the Holy Cross Fathers, the Sisters of St. Francis, the Sisters of the Holy Child, and the Sisters of Charity of the Blessed Virgin Mary.

In 1903, on the recommendation of the Archbishop, the Congregation of the Propaganda divided the Archdiocese, setting up the See of Baker City with jurisdiction over all Oregon east of the Cascade Mountains, and appointing as first bishop of the new diocese the

Most Rev. Charles J. O'Reilly, then pastor of Immaculate Heart Parish, Portland, and editor of the *Catholic Sentinel*. In 1918 Bishop O'Reilly was transferred to the See of Lincoln. He was succeeded as Bishop of Baker by Most Rev. Joseph F. McGrath, formerly pastor of the important parish of St. Patrick in Tacoma. He had been ordained to the priesthood December 21, 1895. His consecration as Bishop of Baker occurred on March 25, 1919. The diocese of Spokane was erected December 17, 1913, and Most Rev. Augustine F. Schinner named first Bishop of Spokane March 18, 1914.

Archbishop Christie observed his silver jubilee in 1924. He was not destined to survive another year. Ill health with which he had been stricken a year earlier returned with serious complications during the early months of 1925. He died at St. Vincent's Hospital on Monday of Holy Week, April 6, 1925. To permit the attendance of other bishops, the funeral was postponed until April 15, when amid a large concourse of sorrowing priests and people the funeral rites were held at the pro-Cathedral and his body interred at Mt. Calvary cemetery. The funeral sermon was preached by Bishop Carroll of Helena, who observed truly: "Not only was the Archbishop known in every diocese of his province, but he was also admired, respected, and loved. His commanding, kingly figure, to which the episcopal robes added comeliness and splendor, made him the cynosure of all eyes, while his stirring yet simple speech, like the language of Holy Writ, with which it was impregnated, was living and effectual and reached the very souls of his hearers. . . . He was the ideal Archbishop. He ruled by love and not by fear. He was a big brother, rather than a father to his suffragan bishops and today they mourn his passing as a personal loss."

The Archbishop had steadily held in abeyance his plan for a worthy Cathedral during the years when he was engaged in building up the parish schools and charitable institutions of the diocese. Following his silver jubilee he felt the time had come for the erection of the Cathedral. The cornerstone was laid on Trinity Sunday, June 8, just two months after the Archbishop's death.

The contest in regard to the Compulsory Public School Attendance Law was the supreme event in his career and we shall close this history with a brief review of that struggle.

The origin of the Oregon anti-Private School Law is to be found in a resolution adopted by the Supreme Council of the Scottish Rite Masons of the Southern Jurisdiction for the United States in May, 1920. The resolution said:

"Resolved, That we recognize and proclaim our belief in the free and compulsory education of the children of our nation in public primary schools supported by public taxation, upon which all children shall attend and be instructed in the English language only, without regard to race or creed, as the only sure foundation for the perpetuation and preservation of our free institutions, guaranteed by the Constitution of the United States. . . . "

This resolution was also adopted by the Grand Lodge of Oregon, A. F. and A. M., in June, 1920. A bill drawn with a view to implementing this resolution was initiated in 1922 by prominent Masons and the petition was circulated for signatures by the various Masonic lodges throughout the state. The bill was offered as an amendment to the existing compulsory school law of the state (not to the state Constitution) and provided in effect that parents should send all children in Oregon between the ages of eight and sixteen years to the public schools, under penalty of fine and imprisonment.

The proposed amendment was ardently espoused by the Ku Klux Klan, at that time nearing the crest of its influence in Oregon. Mr. Pierce, candidate for governor on the Democratic ticket, made the cause his own. In general, the Methodist, Baptist, and Campbellite churches (the most numerous Protestant bodies in Oregon) were active in the Klan campaign. In general the Episcopalian, Presbyterian and Lutheran people opposed it. Nine-tenths of the children in Oregon not attending state schools were in Catholic schools. Consequently the bill was supported by all anti-Catholics whose prejudices eclipsed their intelligence. Under the direction of Archbishop Christie the Catholic forces were organized against the measure and energetically pursued a campaign of enlightenment. The Catholic population of Oregon is about 8 percent of the total. The measure was carried in November, 1922, by a popular vote of 115,506 to 103,685, a majority of 11,821 votes. Considering these conditions, the work of the Friends of Freedom in Education will be seen to have been very effective. While the law was passed in November, 1922, it was not to become effective until September, 1926.

At once the Archbishop organized legal opposition to the law. The financing of the case was assumed by the National Catholic Welfare Conference. The Sisters of the Holy Names, who have conducted schools in Oregon since 1859, brought suit in the Federal District Court seeking an injunction on the ground that the law was unconstitutional. The case was argued in Portland, January 15, 1924, John P. Kavanaugh, distinguished attorney of Portland, making the principal argument for the Sisters. Judge Wolverton wrote the decision of the Court holding that "the absolute right of these schools to teach the grammar grades and the right of parents to engage them to instruct their children is within the liberty of the Fourteenth Amendment." "The melting pot idea applied to the common schools of the state as an incentive for the adoption of this act is an extravagance in simile," observed Judge Wolverton.

Governor Pierce appealed from the decision of the Federal District Court and the case was argued in the Supreme Court of the United States on March 17, 1925, Hon. Wm. Guthrie appearing with Judge Kavanaugh in defense of the Sisters. The unanimous decision of the Supreme Court, written by Associate Justice McReynolds, was delivered June 1, 1925, upholding the decision of the lower court and declaring the act unconstitutional. The Court summarized the Sisters' case as follows:

> "The enactment conflicts with the right of parents to choose schools where their children will receive appropriate mental and religious training; the right of the child to influence of the parents' choice of a school, the right of schools and teachers therein to engage in a useful business or profession and is accordingly repugnant to the Constitution and void; and further, that unless enforcement of the measure is enjoined the corporation's business and property will suffer irreparable injury.
>
> "Appellees (the Sisters) are engaged in a kind of undertaking not inherently harmful, but long regarded as useful and meritorious. Certainly there is nothing in the present records to indicate that they failed to discharge their obligations to patrons, students, or the state. And there are no peculiar circumstances or present emergencies which demand extraordinary measures relative to primary education.

"Under the doctrine of Meyer vs. Nebraska, 262 U. S. 390, we think it entirely plain that the act of 1922 unreasonably interferes with the liberty of parents and guardians to direct the upbringing and education of children under their control. As often heretofore pointed out, rights guaranteed by the Constitution may not be abridged by legislation which has no reasonable relation to some purpose within the competency of the state. The fundamental theory of liberty upon which all governments in this Union repose excludes any general power of the state to standardize its children by forcing them to accept instruction from public teachers only. The child is not the mere creature of the state; those who nurture him and direct his destiny have the right, coupled with the high duty, to recognize and prepare him for additional obligations."

The decision of the Supreme Court in the Oregon School Case was a fitting close to the quarter of a century of zealous labor for Christian education on the part of Archbishop Christie. His life work was the expression of his conviction that the child has a supernatural destiny and his education is incomplete without religion. "The child is not the mere creature of the state," said the United States Supreme Court.

THE HIERARCHY OF THE OREGON PROVINCE

ARCHDIOCESE OF PORTLAND IN OREGON
(Created Archdiocese of Oregon City, July 24, 1846;
present title given by papal decree September 26, 1928)

Most Rev. Francis Norbert Blanchet, consecrated July 25, 1845, Bishop of Drasa and first Vicar Apostolic of Oregon; named Archbishop of Oregon City, July 24, 1846, when vicariate was made an ecclesiastical province; resigned 1880; died June 18, 1883.

Most Rev. Charles John Seghers, consecrated June 29, 1873, Bishop of Vancouver Island; coadjutor Archbishop of Oregon City, December 10, 1878; Archbishop, December 20, 1880; resigned 1884 and was transferred to Vancouver Island; died November 28, 1886.

Most Rev. William H. Gross, C. SS. R., consecrated April 27, 1873, Bishop of Savannah, Georgia; promoted to Oregon City, February 1, 1885; died November 14, 1898.

Most Rev. Alexander Christie, consecrated June 29, 1898, Bishop of Vancouver Island; promoted to Oregon City, February 12, 1899; died April 6, 1925.

Most Rev. Edward D. Howard, consecrated Bishop of Isauria and Bishop Auxiliary of Davenport, Iowa, April 8, 1924. Promoted to the See of Oregon City, April 30, 1926.

DIOCESE OF BAKER CITY
(Established in 1903)

Most Rev. Charles J. O'Reilly, consecrated first Bishop of Baker City, August 25, 1903; transferred to Lincoln, Nebraska, March 20, 1918; died February 4, 1923.

Most Rev. Joseph F. McGrath, consecrated March 25, 1919.

DIOCESE OF BOISE
(Established as a Vicariate Apostolic March 3, 1868, erected a Diocese August 25, 1893)

Most Rev. Louis Lootens, consecrated Bishop of Castabala, and first Vicar Apostolic of Idaho, August 9, 1868; resigned 1876; died January 13, 1898. (From 1876 to 1885, the Vicariate was administered by the Archbishop of Oregon City.)

Most Rev. Alphonse Joseph Glorieux, consecrated Bishop of Apollonia, and second Vicar Apostolic of Idaho, April 19, 1885; named first Bishop of Boise, August 26, 1893; died August 25, 1917.

Most Rev. Daniel Mary Gorman, consecrated May 1, 1918; died June 9, 1927.

Most Rev. Edward Joseph Kelly, consecrated March 6, 1928.

DIOCESE OF GREAT FALLS
(Erected May 18, 1904)

Most Rev. Mathias C. Lenihan, consecrated first Bishop of Great Falls, September 21, 1904; resigned January 18, 1930; created titular Archbishop of Preslavo, February 14, 1930.

Most Rev. Edwin V. O'Hara, consecrated October 28, 1930.

DIOCESE OF HELENA

(Established as Vicariate Apostolic of Montana in 1883, erected as Diocese of Helena, March 7, 1884)

Most Rev. John B. Brondel, consecrated Bishop of Vancouver Island, December 14, 1879; appointed Vicar Apostolic of Montana, April 7, 1883; Bishop of Helena, March 7, 1884; died November 3, 1903.

Most Rev. John P. Carroll, consecrated December 21, 1904; died November 4, 1925.

Most Rev. George F. Finnigan, C. S. C., consecrated August 1, 1927; died August 14, 1932.

Most Rev. Ralph L. Hayes, consecrated September 21, 1933; resigned to become Rector of North American College, Rome, September 11, 1935.

Most Rev. Joseph M. Gilmore, consecrated, February 19, 1936.

DIOCESE OF SEATTLE

(Established as Diocese of Nesqually May 31, 1850, name changed to Seattle September 11, 1907)

Most Rev. Augustine Magloire Blanchet, consecrated Bishop of Walla Walla, September 27, 1846; transferred to Nesqually, May 31, 1850; resigned 1879, named Bishop of Ibora; died February 25, 1887.

Most Rev. Aegidius Junger, consecrated October 28, 1879; died December 26, 1895.

Most Rev. Edward John O'Dea, consecrated September 8, 1896; died December 25, 1932.

Most Rev. Gerald Shaughnessy, S. M., consecrated September 19, 1933.

DIOCESE OF SPOKANE
(Erected December 17, 1913)

Most Rev. Augustine F. Schinner, consecrated Bishop of Superior, Wisconsin, July 25, 1905; resigned January 15, 1913; named first Bishop of Spokane, March 18, 1914; resigned December 17, 1925; named titular Bishop of Sala; died February 7, 1937.

Most Rev. Charles D. White, consecrated February 24, 1927.

VICARIATE APOSTOLIC OF ALASKA
(Established as a Prefecture Apostolic July 17, 1894, erected into a Vicariate Apostolic December 22, 1922)

Rev. Paschal Tosi, S. J., Prefect-Apostolic of Alaska, July 17, 1894, resigned 1897.

Rev. John B. Rene, S. J., Prefect-Apostolic, 1897, resigned 1904.

Most Rev. Joseph Raphael Crimont, S. J., appointed Prefect-Apostolic, March 28, 1904; named Vicar Apostolic February 15, 1917; consecrated titular Bishop of Ammaedera, July 25, 1917.

Most Rev. Walter J. Fitzgerald, S. J., consecrated co-adjutor to the Vicar Apostolic of Alaska, February 24, 1939.

DIOCESE OF WALLA WALLA
(Erected July 24, 1846)

Most Rev. Augustine Magloire Blanchet, consecrated September 27, 1846; transferred to Nesqually, May 31, 1850.

(The Diocese of Walla Walla was administered by the Archbishop of Oregon City from 1850 until its suppression in 1853.)

DIOCESE OF VANCOUVER ISLAND
(Erected July 24, 1846; name changed to Victoria September 6, 1904; part of ecclesiastical province of Oregon until 1908)

Most Rev. Modeste Demers, consecrated November 30, 1847 (first episcopal consecration in Pacific Northwest); died July 27, 1871.

Most Rev. Charles John Seghers, consecrated June 29, 1873; Coadjutor Archbishop of Oregon City, December 10, 1878; Archbishop December 20, 1880; resigned 1884; reappointed Bishop of Vancouver Island in 1885; died November 28, 1886.

Most Rev. John Baptist Brondel, consecrated December 14, 1879; transferred to Vicariate Apostolic of Montana in 1883; Bishop of Helena in 1884; died November 3, 1903.

Most Rev. J. N. Lemmens, consecrated August 5, 1888; died August 10, 1897.

Most Rev. Alexander Christie, consecrated June 29, 1898; promoted to Archiepiscopal See of Oregon City, February 12, 1899; died April 6, 1925.

Most Rev. Bertram Orth, consecrated June 10, 1900; promoted to Archiepiscopal See of Vancouver Island, June 25, 1903; resigned June 25, 1908. Appointed titular Archbishop of Amasea, October 1, 1908.

(With the close of the administration of Archbishop Orth the Diocese of Vancouver Island ceased to be a part of the ecclesiastical province of Oregon.)

BIBLIOGRAPHY

The following list contains the principal sources and authorities which have been consulted in the preparation of this volume.

Archives of the Archdiocese of Oregon City

Manuscript Journals of Archbishops F. N. Blanchet and Charles John Seghers. Letters of early missionaries, official papers, etc.

Bailey, Margaret Jewett

The Grains; or Passages in the Life of Ruth Rover. (Portland, 1854.) Photostatic copy in State Library, Salem, Oregon, beginning with Chapter XIV.

Bagley, Clarence B.

In the Beginning (Chapter LXIII, of Pioneer Reminiscences of Puget Sound, by Ezra Meeker). Seattle, 1905.

Bancroft, H. H.

History of the Northwest Coast (San Francisco, 1884.) Idem: History of Oregon (San Francisco, 1886-1888).

Barrows, Rev. Wm.

Oregon; the Struggle for Possession (American Commonwealth Series). (Houghton, Mifflin & Co., 1883.) Its inclusion in the Commonwealth series gave the book an unmerited reputation and did more to spread the Whitman myth than all other agencies. Barrows was made financial agent of Whitman College, 1887, and held the position until his death in 1891.

Beadle, H. M.

American Catholic Historical Researches. October, 1899, pp. 187-197. Whitman Legend. Reaches same conclusion as Bourne.

Blanchet, Most Rev. F. N.

Letters on the Catholic Indian Missions of Oregon. (Portland, 1871.) Address of the Catholic Clergy of Oregon on President Grant's Indian Policy. (Portland, 1874.)

Blanchet, F. N.

The Key to the Catholic Ladder. (New York, 1859.) — Pastoral letter concerning the two first Dogmatic Constitutions of the Vatican Council. (From out the Flamminian Gate.) Portland, 1870. — Pastoral for the Lent of 1876. — Pastoral Letter and Conciliary Discourse, also Address to Pope Pius IX. (1871.)

Blanchet, F. N.

Jubilee of Fiftieth Anniversary of the Ordination to the Priesthood of Most Rev. F. N. Blanchet. (Portland, July 18, 1869.) Pamphlet, p. 15.

Blanchet, F. N.

Historical Sketches of the Catholic Church in Oregon. (Catholic Sentinel Press, Portland, Ore., 1878; new edition, Ferndale, Wash., 1910.)

Blanchet, F. N.

Pastoral Letter promulgating the Jubilee. (Portland, 1865.) — Historical Notes and Reminiscences. (Portland, 1883.) — Life and Labors of Most Rev. F. N. Blanchet with funeral sermons by Most Rev. Chas. John Seghers. (Portland, 1883.)

Blanchet, Rev. F. X.

Dix Ans sur la Côte du Pacifique. (Quebec, 1873.)

Bolduc, Rev. J. Z. B.

Mission de la Colombie; Lettre et Journal. (Quebec, 1844.)

Bourne, Edward Gaylord

Essays in Historical Criticism. (New York, 1901.) The Whitman Legend, pp. 1-109. — (Independently of Marshall, Bourne arrives at the conclusion that the Whitman Legend is wholly mythical.)

Brouillet, Very Rev. J. B. A.

Vicar General of the Diocese of Walla Walla. Authentic Account of the Murder of Dr. Whitman. (2nd ed., Portland, 1869.) Also published unintentionally by Ross Browne as part of his Report in Executive Document No. 38, House of Representatives, 35th Congress, 1st Session, dated San Francisco, Dec. 4, 1857. Brouillet's pamphlet was written in 1848; published in 1853.

Burnett, Peter Hardeman

Recollections and Opinions of an Old Pioneer. (New York, 1880.) — Id., The Path Which Led a Protestant Lawyer to the Catholic Church. New Edition, St. Louis, 1910.

Catholic Sentinel

(Files 1870-1911). Portland, Oregon.

Catholic World Magazine

February, 1872, pp. 665-682. Contains critical examination of Spalding's pamphlet issued as Senate Document.

Chaparro, R. P.

Noticias sobre la Provincia Ecclesiastica de Oregon. (Valparaiso, Chili, 1856.) A translation from the French, published during the South American tour of Archbishop Blanchet.

Chittenden and Richardson

DeSmet's Life and Travels, 4 vols. (Complete edition of DeSmet's letters. Critical.) Harpers.

Clark, Robert Carlton, Ph. D.

History of the Willamette Valley, Oregon. (Chicago, 1927.)

Clarke, Richard H.

Lives of Deceased Bishops of the United States, Vol. III. (New York, 1888.)

De Baets, l'Abbé Maurice

Msgr. Seghers, L'Apôtre de Alaska. (Ghent and Paris, 1896.)

Drury, Clifford Merrill, Ph. D.
Marcus Whitman, M. D. (Caldwell, Idaho, 1937.)

Dugas, l'Abbé G.
Monseigneur Provencher et les Missions de la Rivière-Rouge. (Montreal, 1889.)

Garraghan, Gilbert J., S. J., Ph. D.
The Jesuits of the Middle United States. (New York, 1938.)

Gleanings of Fifty Years; A Sister of the Holy Names
Portland, 1909. A most interesting account of the work of the Sisters of the Holy Names of the Oregon Province.

Guilday, Peter
A History of the Councils of Baltimore. (New York, 1932.)

Holman, Frederick V.
Dr. John McLoughlin, the Father of Oregon. (Cleveland, 1907.) A classic monograph on early Oregon history.

In Harvest Fields by Sunset Shores: A Sister of Notre Dame
(San Francisco.)

Johnson, Robert C.
John McLoughlin, Patriarch of the Northwest. (Portland, 1935.)

Kane, Paul
Wanderings of an Artist among the Indians of North America. (London, 1859, p. 455.) — At Whitman's Mission, July 22, 1847. Invited Whitman to Fort Walla Walla with McBean to avoid danger.

Laveille, E.
Life of Father DeSmet. (Kenedy, New York, 1915.)

MacKay, Douglas
The Honourable Company. (New York, 1936.)

MacLeod, Rev. Xavier D.

Devotion to the Blessed Virgin Mary in North America. New York, 1866. (Chapter XIII contains account of the journey of Sister Renilda and her companions, Sisters of Notre Dame, to Oregon in 1847.)

Mallet, Edmond, LL. B.

The Origin of the Oregon Mission. Art. in U. S. Historical Magazine, Vol. I, No. 1. (January, 1887.) — Memoirs of Archbishop F. N. Blanchet. Unpublished Ms. in the library of l'Union St. Jean-Baptiste d'Amérique, Woonsocket, R. I. (Copy in possession of author of this volume.)

Marshall, William I.

Acquisition of Oregon and the Long Suppressed Evidence about Marcus Whitman, 2 vol. — (Seattle, 1911.) Limited edition printed by subscription. (200 copies.)

Marshall, William I.

History vs. The Whitman Saved Oregon Story. (Chicago, 1894.)

Marshall, Wm. I.

The Hudson's Bay Company's Archives furnish no support to the Whitman Saved Oregon Story. (Chicago, 1905.) A criticism of address by Dwight N. Hillis.

Mesplié, Rev. Toussaint

Petitions and papers praying for relief for acting as Indian agent and negotiator, peace-maker, and chaplain to the United States army. (Miscellaneous Doc., House of Representatives, January 26, 1874.)

Metropolitan Catholic Almanac and Laity's Directory (Baltimore).

De Mofras, M. Duflot

Exploration du territoire de l'Oregon, 2 vols. — (Paris, 1844.) Attaché a la légation de France á Mexico. Second volume tells of Catholic missionaries in Oregon.

Montgomery, Richard

The White-headed Eagle: John McLoughlin, Builder of an Empire. (MacMillan, New York, 1935.)

Morice, Rev. A. G., O. M. I.

History of the Catholic Church in Western Canada, 2 vols. (Toronto, 1910.) — Dictionnaire Historique des Canadiens et des Métis Francais de l'Ouest (Quebec, 1908.)

Notice sur le Territoire et sur à la Mission de l'Oregon suivie de quelques lettres des soeurs de Notre Dame établies à Saint-Paul du Willamette (Bruxelles, 1847). (Letters of the Sisters of Notre Dame, dated at St. Paul, Ore., 1844-5.)

The Notre Dame Quarterly

San Jose, Cal. The Sisters of Notre Dame on the Pacific Coast, 1910-1911.

Oregon Archives

From earliest attempt on the part of the people to form a government to 1849. 1841-1849. (Salem, Ore., 1853.) — Contains address of Canadian citizens of Oregon to the meeting at Champoeg, March 4, 1843, pp. 12-13. Father Accolti's answer about ammunition. Oregon Archives Ms., 156-160.

Oregon American and Evangelical Unionist

Edited by Rev. J. S. Griffin, at Oregon City. Issued semi-monthly. Devoted its pages very largely to giving publicity to Spalding's insane calumnies. The issue of June 7, 1848, contains Burnett's reply to Spalding. August 16, 1848, tells of interception of ammunition by Lieutenant Rodgers.

Oregonian Files

(Portland, 1850 —.)

Palladino, S. J., L. B.

Indian and White in the Northwest or a History of Catholicity in Montana (Baltimore, 1894). (Has given currency to the correct explanation of the visit of the Rocky Mountain Indians to St. Louis in 1831-39.)

Quarterly of the Oregon Historical Association

(Portland, 1900-1911.)

Rapport sur les Missions du Diocése de Québec

(March, 1853.) (Lettre de Msgr. Demers.) (Juin, 1843.) Mission de la Columbie, pp. 22-116. (Juillet, 1847.) Memoire presente a la S. Congregation de la Propaganda sur le territoire de l'Oregon par Mgr. F. N. Blanchet, eveque de Drasa, pp. 1-24. Extraits de diverses lettres de M. Demers.

Rapport sur les Missions du Diocése de Québec

(Mars, 1851). Voyage de l'Eveque de Walla Walla. Rapport de M. Brouillet sur sa Mission de Ste. Ann (p. 39).

Reports of the Board of Indian Commissioners

(Annual, 1869 —.)

Rossi, L'Abbé L.

Six Ans en Amérique (Deuxieme edition, Paris, 1863). The author was at Vancouver, Washington Territory, in 1859.

De St.-Amant, M.

Voyages en Californie, et dans l'Oregon, 1851-52. (Paris, 1854.) St.-Amant sent by ministry of Foreign Affairs of French Republic to California and Oregon to examine with view to French Commerce. The Empire succeeded the Republic. No official report but above book published. "Envoyé du gouvernement Francaise, 1851-2."

Schafer, Joseph

History of the Pacific Northwest. (New York, 1935.)

Shea, John Gilmary
> History of the Catholic Church in the United States. Vol. IV. deals with Oregon. (New York, 1892.)

Snowden, Clinton A.
> History of Washington, 4 vols. (New York, 1909.) An excellent work. The first two volumes deal with the pioneer history of the Oregon Country.

Spalding, Rev. H. H.
> Senate Executive Document 37, 41st Congress, 3rd Session. (Contains Spalding's version of the Whitman affair.)

Tassé, Joseph
> Les Canadiens de l'Ouest, 2 vols. (Montreal, 1878.) — Gabriel Franchère, Vol. II, p. 261, ff. — Pierre Chrysologue Pambrun, Vol. II, p. 299, ff. — Joseph Larocque, Vol. II., p. 321, ff.

Transactions of the Oregon Pioneer Association
> Salem, 1874-1887.

Van der Donckt
> Founders of the Church in Idaho. American Eccl. Review, 1905.

Van der Heyden, Rev. J.
> Msgr. Adrian J. Croquet, Indian Missionary. (Series of articles in the Records of the American Catholic Historical Society of Philadelphia, 1905.)

Victor, Frances Fuller
> The Early Indian Wars of Oregon. (Salem, Ore., 1894.)

White, Dr. Elijah
> Ten Years in Oregon; Travels and Adventures of Dr. E. White and Lady, West of the Rocky Mts. (Ithaca, N. Y., 1848.) Dr. White had been medical missionary at Methodist mission in Willamette Valley 1838-40. Sub-Indian agent for Oregon, 1842-45. Only U. S. official residing in Oregon before 1849.

Wilkes Exploring Expedition
> Vol. IV., p. 348 seq., tells of Blanchet's opposition to provisional government and justifies it.

INDEX

229

PUBLISHERS' NOTICES:

"The most satisfactory general account of the history of the Church in Oregon proper, is that by Bishop Edwin V. O'Hara, *Catholic History of Oregon,* Portland, 1925, which is really a revision brought down to 1925 of the same author's *The Pioneer Catholic History of Oregon,* Portland, 1911. In the preparation of these works Bishop O'Hara had access to the manuscript materials in the Portland archdiocesan archives. The introductory chapters in both volumes treat of Catholic beginnings in Washington and British Columbia as well as in the present state of Oregon." Thomas F. O'Connor, M. A., *A Century of Catholicism in the Oregon Country,* HISTORICAL RECORDS AND STUDIES, of the United States Catholic Historical Society, Vol. 29 (1938).

* * * * * *

"The best history for the general reader is O'Hara, E. V., *Catholic History of Oregon,* Portland, 1916. This work includes the Jesuit missions and recent history." George W. Fuller, *A History of the Pacific Northwest,* page 361, New York, 1931.